AGING:

God's Challenge to Church & Synagogue

Richard H. Gentzler, Jr.
Donald F. Clingan

Foreword by Rabbi Richard F. Address

DISCIPLESHIP RESOURCES
MATERIALS FOR GROWTH IN CHRISTIAN FAITH & LIFE
— NASHVILLE, TENNESSEE —

P.O. BOX 840 • NASHVILLE, TN 37202 • PHONE (615) 340-7068

Images © 1996 PhotoDisc, Inc.

Library of Congress Catalog Card No. 95-69951

ISBN 0-88177-144-9

Unless otherwise indicated, all Scripture passages are from the New Revised Standard Version, Copyright 1989, Division of Christian Education of the National Council of the Churches of Christ in the United States of America.

DR144

CONTENTS

FOREWORD

As the Book of Deuteronomy concludes, we are told that
Moses lived to be 120 years old before he died and that his eyes
were "unimpaired" and "his vigor had not abated" (Deut. 34:27).
This simple phrase can teach us much about the age of gerontology that we are poised to enter. The Torah, in its usual wisdom and
often prophetic point of view, reminds us that while death is part
of who we are, we must not lose the sense of wonder, mystery, and
celebration of our own life—a celebration which will allow us no
end to our own vigor and vision.

We are about to enter the era of so-called "baby-boomer" gerontology. If we look at informed speculation as well as published
studies, it seems we are about to confront an age in which the
rules of how we in society see and relate to older adults will
change dramatically. For us in the religious community this hidden
revolution is of even greater importance. How synagogues,
churches, and other religious organizations can meet the challenges of the new older adult population forms the focus of
Richard Gentzler's and Donald Clingan's work. Indeed, it serves as
a necessary bridge into a programmatic and theological arena that

is just beginning to become evident.

Indicative of how the challenge of aging can be met is an emphasis that mirrors the new older adult. This is an emphasis on empowerment—a sense that I, as an individual, should have and can have a greater say in how I live my life. It can be argued that this will be one of the great legacies of the post-World War II American generation. Its effect on a generation that will soon confront its individual and collective mortality is a source of great tension and challenge. This empowerment stands ready to manifest a profound sense of challenge on the part of the synagogue and church. Within this challenge is the understanding that the increasing number of older adult members will require new and different responses to their growing personal independence and spiritual evolution.

Key to being able to respond to this sense of empowerment will be the interconnection between the concepts of covenant, faith, and community. These values will be expressed by individuals in their search for personal meaning and by churches and synagogues in their drive to provide vehicles through which these values may be achieved. Thus, the meeting ground for the spiritual component of the new older adult should be the synagogue or church, where these values find expression.

It is in the harvest of life that life's fullness and richness are revealed. This richness is often misunderstood as seeing our own life in the context of a greater Power. This covenant relationship with God (a partnership which allows us to seek our individual meaning in terms of transcendent truth) provides opportunities for a renewal and expression of faith. It is through this exploration of personal meaning within a larger context that the older adult can be empowered by church or synagogue to find meaning and purpose within the building of community.

As a new age of older adulthood dawns, the synagogue and church have the potential to be the foundation upon which older adults can find renewed vision and vigor. Truly, by responding to the challenges before them, religious communities can be the source that empowers this population to find new and dynamic expressions to personal searches of meaning and purpose. Respond creatively to these new challenges, and we harvest a generation of spiritually liberated souls.

What emerges throughout this book is the realization that the church and synagogue have to understand that a potential golden age of spiritual growth and evolution awaits. This will require, in many cases, substantive changes in our institutional psyches. Yet, as Gentzler and Clingan remind us, the future is very much at hand and the sheer numbers and cultural reality of what is upon us will force our religious communal organizations to react.

This book throws down the challenge for those organizations and institutions to be proactive in their responses to the emerging changes within the older adult community. It reinforces the foundation of building a community based on faith and our sacred relationship with God. It challenges the church and the synagogue, as well as the older adult, to embrace this new and exciting time of life as one of potential and possibility.

Ultimately our churches and synagogues are about individual people, people of all ages, who freely choose to affiliate. In a very real sense they are people who place their souls into our keeping in order to create a community and receive a sense of spiritual growth and personal meaning. This is our challenge! A wonderful task awaits us as new generations of older adults stand poised to engage us. Better educated, living longer, more independent, the emerging older adult population will draw from its own social and cultural journey to question and search as never before as to their own meaning and purpose. This is where we shall meet them.

For the basic human questions remain questions of personal meaning and ultimate purpose in the face of mortality. How we respond will go a long way in determining the moral and spiritual foundation of the next century. Using *Aging: God's Challenge to Church and Synagogue* as textbook, programming manual, and resource guide will help fashion a variety of needed responses drawn from communities of faith. It is this faith which will ultimately remain the foundation of our commitment to covenant and serve as the impetus to create communities of caring souls.

Rabbi Richard F. Address
Director, Committees on Older Adults and Bioethics,
Union of American Hebrew Congregations

PREFACE

The authors first met in Lemoyne, Pennsylvania, in a seminar on ministry with the aging. Richard Gentzler (Rick) was a young, enthusiastic United Methodist pastor who was working on his Doctor of Ministry degree at Boston University School of Theology in the area of pastoral counseling and gerontology.

Donald Clingan (Don), an ordained minister of the Christian Church (Disciples of Christ), had served as the founding president and first executive director of the National Interfaith Coalition on Aging, Inc. At the time of the seminar, he was executive director of the National Center on Ministry with the Aging, sponsored by the National Benevolent Association of the Christian Church (Disciples of Christ), and Christian Theological Seminary, Indianapolis, Indiana, with headquarters at the seminary. In this capacity, he was conducting seminars on ministry with the aging for his denomination and many other faiths all over the United States.

Clingan was also the author of an interfaith congregational guidebook, *Aging Persons in the Community of Faith*, which was used as the seminar text, and had received his Doctor of Ministry degree from Christian Theological Seminary in ministry with the aging and Christian ethics. He had also received a Graduate Certificate in Gerontology at the University of Oregon Center for Gerontology and had involved himself in training at the New England Center for Gerontology at the University of New Hampshire, Durham.

After continued successful pastoral ministry, Rick was invited to serve as the director of educational ministries with older adults and later the director of the Office of Adult Ministries for The General Board of Discipleship of The United Methodist Church. In this capacity, he authored a manual, *Designing a Ministry By, With, and For Older Adults*, and has been conducting workshops for leaders of older adult ministries throughout the United States.

Meanwhile, the National Center on Ministry with the Aging was closed for lack of funding and Don returned to the pastorate, serving as senior minister of the First Christian Church, Springfield, Illinois. He retired in 1992, then became active again in national aging work and served as membership chairman of the National Interfaith Coalition on Aging (NICA), now a unit of the National Council on the Aging, Inc. He also served as an Illinois delegate to the 1995 White House Conference on Aging, having been a delegate to the 1971 conference and an official observer to the 1981 conference.

Rick and Don renewed their friendship as members of the Delegate Council (board) of the National Interfaith Coalition on Aging and have joined together in the authorship of this new book directed to help Jewish and Christian leaders and congregations in effective ministry with the aging. Since aging is a life-long process, this book speaks principally to those persons whom we have defined as older adults.

In this co-authorship, we are grateful to the following persons for their support and wisdom shared to make this effort reality:

- To our spouses, Marilyn Gentzler and Jacquie Clingan, for their undergirding support and love.

- To Ann Woodmore, Sheila Maxwell, David Hazlewood, and the editors of Discipleship Resources for their editorial assistance.

- To the many reviewers for their contributions to this book and to the field of gerontology and ministry with older adults. These reviewers include: Richard F. Address, Sharon Anderson, Dosia Carlson, Marvin W. Cropsey, Chester E. Custer, Miriam Dunson, Harry J. Ekstam, William L. Howse III, George Knight, Elizabeth Knowles-Bagwell, Jane C. Lawrence, Polly Leland-Mayer, Jan L. McGilliard, Milton E. Owens, Susanne Paul, Eleanor L. Richardson, Henry C. Simmons, and Linda J. Vogel.

INTRODUCTION

Why should the church and synagogue be concerned about ministry with the aging?

When this question is raised, the story of Mrs. Smith comes to mind. This woman was brought to the adult services division of the Philadelphia Department of Public Welfare by the police. They had found her wandering the streets of the city, talking incoherently, not remembering her name or knowing where she lived. They hoped the Department of Public Welfare could help this poor woman.

Mrs. Smith was seated at the desk of a social worker, who tried to bring her into reality. Vicky Peralta, director of the adult services division, saw this woman and realized that Mrs. Smith had been one of the persons whom she had known at the Philadelphia Center for Older Adults when Vicky was its program director.

Vicky ran up to Mrs. Smith, calling out her name. "Mrs. Smith, do you remember me? I am Vicky Peralta." But Mrs. Smith just looked blankly into the distance.

"Mrs. Smith," said Vicky, "don't you remember our good times together at the Philadelphia center?" But still Mrs. Smith had no glimmer of recognition in her eyes.

Finally Vicky noticed that Mrs. Smith held tightly in her hands her most precious possession—a Bible. With this observation, Vicky asked Mrs. Smith: "What are your favorite Scriptures?"

This incoherent woman, who did not know where she lived or who she was, quoted without mistake:

> *The Lord is my shepherd,*
> *I shall not want.*
> *He makes me lie down in green pastures,*
> *He leads me beside still waters;*
> *He restores my soul.*

And she went on until she had completed the entire Twenty-third Psalm. Then she began to quote John 3:16:

> *For God so loved the world that he gave his only son, so that everyone who believes in him may not perish, but may have eternal life.*

For this lost woman, who knew not where she was or who she was, the Scriptures were her only touch with reality.

Our relationship with God *is* important to the wholeness of our lives. Our spiritual well-being as we grow older *is* an imperative in our lives. Therefore, *God's challenge to church and synagogue becomes apparent when it comes to ministry with older adults. God calls us to become as effective as possible in this ministry.*

The Purpose of This Book

For this reason, it is our hope that this book's message may help clergy, laity, educators, and older adults of church and synagogue to face more effectively God's challenge of ministry with the aging, most particularly with older adults. This ministry should include enabling older adults to make their own decisions regarding their future, insofar as they are able.

Congregations want help in the important, yet too-often-over-looked ministry with older adults. It is obvious that a source is needed which goes deeper than previous publications into the subject of aging and the vital relationship of older adults to church and synagogue. Therefore, this book will provide key information on the following topics:

1. An exploration of Aging and Older Adults (Chapter 1).
2. A discussion of Spiritual Needs of Older Adults (Chapter 2).
3. An examination of a Theology of Aging (Chapter 3).
4. Tips on Getting Started in Older Adult Ministries (Chapter 4).
5. Guidance on the Who, What, and How of Leadership in Older Adult Ministries (Chapter 5).
6. A cafeteria of Program Directions and Models for Older Adult Ministries (Chapter 6).
7. A look at Caregiving: A Role of Church and Synagogue (Chapter 7).
8. Exploring opportunities for Uniting Generations (Chapter 8).
9. Guidance for lifting up the means by which Congregations and Communities Working Together may develop a creative teamwork in older adult ministries (Chapter 9).
10. A look at Challenges of the Future in ministry with older adults (Chapter 10).
11. A Postscript on God's Challenge Requires a New Commitment.

So let us begin our adventure together.

Chapter 1

BUILDING A
NEW CONCEPT
OF AGING AND
OLDER ADULTS

One of the difficulties in considering aging is defining the term. If we use the word *aging* primarily as a description for older adults, we limit the word. Aging begins at conception and continues throughout all of life. Every creature, every living thing, ages. The only alternative to aging is death.

Likewise, if we use the word *aged* as a descriptive meaning for older adults, we imply that at some point in time, people stop aging. If older adults are "the aged," then we falsely assume that the aging process has ceased and that older adults have stopped changing, growing, and learning.

Even the term *old* is relative to one's life situation. For example, a sixteen-year-old girl may seem quite old to her ten-year-old brother. A twenty-two-year-old college graduate may be thought of as "old" by his thirteen-year-old cousin. Even an eighty-seven-year-old nursing home resident might view her ninety-year-old roommate as "old" in comparison to her own age!

How then do we describe aging older persons? Sometimes older people are described as "seniors," "senior citizens," "the elder-

ly," or "golden agers." Sometimes, however, they are described in
less flattering terms such as "greedy geezers," "old maid," "hag," or
"dirty old man." Maggie Kuhn, founder of the Gray Panthers, stated
that our society often views older people as "wrinkled babies."
Since the focus of this book is on "adults" who are "older," it seems
quite appropriate for us to use the term *older adult* as a descriptive word for persons in their later years of life. In addition, we
will use the term *older adulthood* to refer to the characteristics of
older adults.

When Is Older Adulthood Attained?

When does a person become an "older adult"? Does a person
suddenly wake up one day and realize, "I am an older adult?" Does
a person have to pass a test, verifying authenticity in claiming the
right to be an older adult? Does a medical doctor, the government,
or some other entity signify the inevitable and place a stamp of
approval, proclaiming that one has reached older adulthood? How
do we determine who is an older adult and who is not?

Typically, being an older adult is most often thought of in
terms of *chronological age*. And the chronological age most often
associated with the beginning of older adulthood in the United
States is sixty-five. But is this a valid way of determining older
adulthood? Is everyone an older adult simply because she or he
has reached the age of sixty-five? Will this change as eligibility for
receiving full Social Security benefits creeps upward beyond age
sixty-five?

The U. S. Department of Labor defines an older worker as
anyone who is forty years of age and older. The American
Association of Retired Persons (AARP), with more than thirty-three
million members, identifies persons who are fifty years of age and
over as potential members. Many restaurants, movie theaters, and
transportation companies provide discounted services to persons
fifty-five years of age and older. In addition, many churches and
synagogues have "fifty-five-plus" groups for persons whom they
identify as older adults.

Some gerontologists speak of older adulthood as the "third
age" or describe older adults as being in the "fourth quarter" of life.
Another way of defining older adults using chronological age

would be to place older adulthood into three categories: young-older adult (sixty-five to seventy-four), middle-older adult (seventy-five to eighty-four), and oldest-older adult (eighty-five and above). Certainly, as we will see later in this chapter when we discuss transitions in older adulthood, this last example may be a better way of defining older adulthood.

Chronological age alone, however, doesn't adequately describe older adulthood. We also need to think about the biological, legal, psychological, social, and spiritual ages helping to determine older adulthood.

Biological age refers to the physiological changes that occur as a person ages. For example, as people age they will likely experience sensory losses. Reduced senses are due to the general declining capacity of the sensory system to receive and transmit messages. As a result, increased hearing loss and impaired vision occur as people get older. However, our bodies do not age in place. We may have a young heart, but old lungs. Our respiratory system may function well, but our circulatory system may be a bit "sluggish."

How a person feels may be an important factor in determining one's age. If persons are faced with pain and multiple chronic illnesses, they may feel older than they actually are. On the other hand, if persons have good health, they may feel younger!

In looking at how the legal system defines aging, we become aware that there are a variety of laws in our society that affect aging persons. The *legal age* of someone is determined by the laws of society. For example, in many states, a person is not permitted to drive an automobile until she or he has reached the age of sixteen. Likewise, citizens in the United States are not permitted to vote until they are eighteen years of age. A law affecting older adults has to do with Social Security. Presently, full Social Security benefits are not normally paid until a person is sixty-five years old. Persons born after January 2, 1960, will receive full benefits beginning at the age of sixty-seven.

How old I think I am is associated with *psychological age*. Often, when children are young, they can't wait to grow up. Small children will dress up like Mommy and Daddy and pretend to be adults. This role-playing is significant as preparation for adulthood.

Young people fourteen and fifteen years of age can't wait until they reach sixteen so they can drive a car. Persons sixteen and seventeen years of age are anxiously awaiting eighteen so they can be considered an adult in our society.

As persons grow older, many adults look forward to a specific age when they will be able to retire from the rigors of their jobs. Even in modern times, with the change from retirement to "rehirement," many adults have certain expectations about reaching "retirement age." But there is also another side to psychological age.

Many adults do not see themselves at their chronological age. This impacts their psychological age. Thus, an active seventy-year-old may think of herself or himself as fifty. This is often a result of the negative images we have of aging. Persons don't see themselves at a given age because they perceive age to be something different from the age they actually are. Age denial is inherent in a society that prizes beauty and youth over against wisdom and experience. Inevitably, the mirror may become the real enemy for persons who deny their age!

Social age becomes a reality when we begin to lose friends and family members to death and we look around and see few of our friends and family left. Social age helps us identify our aging not only by the remaining number of friends and family members we now have, but also by the friends we associate with. Classes in churches and synagogues are often age-segregated. Being identified with a particular age group cohort for social and learning activities often suggests that we are seen by others as belonging to this particular group. Enjoying the activities of this age group cohort also signifies our role at this time in life.

Spiritual age refers to the degree of mature faith often associated with older adults. According to the Search Institute, as persons age, they have a greater likelihood of developing mature faith. (Mature faith as defined by the Search Institute consists of a transforming relationship to a loving God and a consistent devotion to serving others.) "Not surprisingly, young adults generally have a lower faith maturity than older adults. While only 16 percent of adults in their twenties have a mature faith, 57 percent of adults over 70 have a mature faith."[1]

While not all older adults have a mature faith, spiritual aging is often associated with the wisdom that experience brings. Many older adults have for the first time in their lives an opportunity to concentrate fully on their relationship with God and to develop their faith. When persons are in young and middle adulthood, time is consumed with work, raising families, and other activities that occupy their time and energy. They may participate in worship on a regular basis, and may even be active in the life of the church or synagogue through study and service.

However, older adulthood often provides the time needed for persons to be "at one" with God. Regular Bible reading, devotional study, and prayer time, as well as being in service to others, are ways that spiritual age helps define older adults.

Clearly, chronological, biological, legal, psychological, social, and spiritual ages are important ways of defining older adults. If just one of these factors is used to describe an older adult, it may not be sufficient. However, when used together, they provide a helpful means for understanding aging and older adults.

Who Are Older Adults?

The older adult population in the United States (persons sixty-five years of age and older) numbered 33.2 million in 1994. This number represented 12.7 percent of the total population or about one in eight Americans. Since 1900, the percentage of Americans sixty-five years of age and older has tripled (from 4.1 percent in 1900 to 12.7 percent in 1994), and the number has increased ten times (from 3.1 million to 33.2 million).[2]

In 1900, when the sixty-five-and-over age group represented only four percent of the total U. S. population, children and teenagers made up forty percent of the population. In 1994, however, the sixty-five-and-over age group represented about 12.7 percent of the population, while children and teenagers made up only twenty-four percent of the total U. S. population. By the year 2030, there will be proportionately more older adults than young people in the population: between twenty to twenty-two percent of the population will be sixty-five and older, and approximately nineteen percent will be children and teenagers.[3] (See Figure 1.)

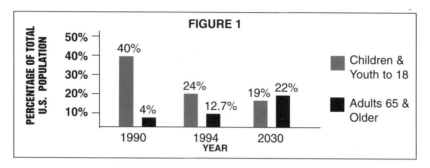

While we are becoming a society composed largely of adults, the older adult population is expected to continue to grow in the future. As a result of better health care, nutrition, and job safety, many more Americans are living into older adulthood. Every day in the United States 5,600 people celebrate their sixty-fifth birthday, and on each given day 4,550 persons, sixty-five years or older, die. The result is a net increase of 1,050 older adults per day. By 2030, there will be about seventy million older persons, more than twice their number in 1994.[4]

Many churches and synagogues are also experiencing an increased percentage of membership in older adults. This is due, in part, to younger and middle adults choosing not to participate in congregations. Like society, faith communities are "graying," too, but at an even faster rate than society. It isn't unusual to find many local churches and synagogues having an older adult membership that represents over sixty percent of their total membership, with some even higher! Even religious bodies and judicatories at all levels are experiencing an increasing percentage of older adults.

Let's look at some of the demographic information associated with older adults in our society.

Sex ratio. The ratio of women to men varies dramatically with age. In 1994, the number of females to males who were sixty-five years of age and over was 19.7 million women compared to 13.5 million men. Older women outnumber older men by three to two. As age increases, the percentage of older women compared to older men continues to grow. For persons eighty-five years of age and older, there are thirty-nine men for every one hundred women.[5]

6

Marital status. In 1994, older men were nearly twice as likely to be married as older women—seventy-seven percent of men, forty-three percent of women. While most older men remain married until they die, nearly half (forty-seven percent) of older women are widowed.[6]

There are several reasons for this disparity. Men have a shorter average life expectancy (78.4 years for women and 71.5 years for men) and thus tend to die before their wives. In addition, men tend to marry women younger than themselves. Finally, men who lose a spouse through death or divorce are more likely to remarry than are women in the same situation.

Race and ethnicity. In 1994, about fourteen percent of people age sixty-five and above were minorities—eight percent were Black, two percent were Asian or Pacific Islander, and less than one percent were American Indian or Native Alaskan. Persons of Hispanic origin (who may be of any race) represented four percent of the older population.[7] (See Figure 2.)

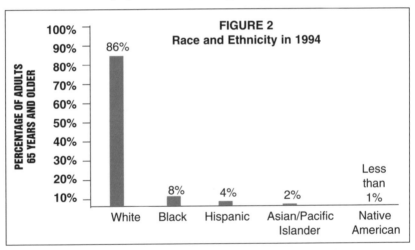

Geographic distribution. In 1994, about half (fifty-two percent) of the persons sixty-five years of age and older lived in nine states: California, Florida, New York, Pennsylvania, Texas, Ohio, Illinois, Michigan, and New Jersey. Each of these states had over one million people sixty-five years of age and older. In fact, California had over three million, while Florida and New York each had over two million. The state with the fewest older adults was Alaska, with approximately 28,000, followed by Wyoming, with 53,000.

The state with the highest percentage of older adults is Florida. Over eighteen percent of the total population of Florida is comprised of persons sixty-five years of age and older. Florida is followed by Pennsylvania, Rhode Island, Iowa, West Virginia, Arkansas, South Dakota, North Dakota, Nebraska, Missouri, and Massachusetts as states with the highest percentage of older adults.[8]

Health status. Contrary to popular opinion, most older people view their health positively. According to results of the 1989 health interview survey conducted by the National Center for Health Statistics, nearly seventy-one percent of older adults living in the community described their health as excellent, very good, or good. Less than twenty-nine percent of the older adults polled described their health as fair or poor.[9]

The pattern of illness and disease has changed in the past ninety-five years. Acute conditions were predominant at the turn of the century, while chronic conditions are now the prevalent health problem for older adults. While three-fourths of all deaths among older adults are from heart disease, cancer, and stroke, chronic conditions increase rapidly with age. More than four out of five older adults have at least one chronic condition. The leading chronic conditions are arthritis, hypertension, heart disease, and hearing impairments.[10]

Living arrangements. In 1994, the majority (sixty-eight percent) of noninstitutionalized older adults lived in a family setting. Approximately eighty-one percent of older men and fifty-eight percent of older women live in families. Of this percentage, seventy-five percent of older men and forty-one percent of older women live with spouses.[11] (See Figure 3.)

Noninstitutionalized older adults living alone comprise nearly thirty percent of all older people. In 1994, they represented sixteen percent of older men and forty percent of older women.[12] They also constitute one of the most vulnerable and impoverished segments of our society. They have lower incomes than older married couples, particularly if they are over age eighty-five, women, or

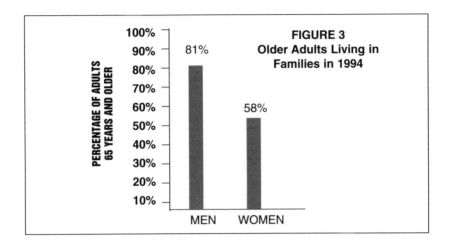

FIGURE 3
Older Adults Living in
Families in 1994

members of minority groups. In addition, older adults who live alone may have chronic health problems that make it difficult for them to remain independent. While family and friends may provide assistance with daily living needs, many older adults who live alone have no one to help them.

Poverty status. Older adults (sixty-five years of age and older) are no more likely than other adults (ages eighteen through sixty-four) to be poor. The poverty rate for older adults in 1994 was 11.7 percent, while the poverty rate for adults (ages eighteen through sixty-four) was 11.9 percent. This means that roughly one in eight older adults live in poverty. One of every ten (ten percent) White older adults was poor in 1994, compared to about one-fourth (twenty-seven percent) of Black older adults and one-fourth (twenty-three percent) of Hispanic older adults.[13] (See Figure 4.)

Older women in 1994 had a higher poverty rate (fifteen percent) than older men (seven percent). Likewise, older persons living alone or with nonrelatives were more likely to be poor (twenty-three percent) than were older persons living in families (six percent).[14]

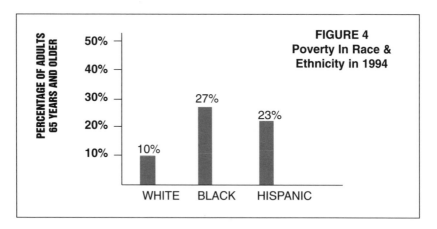

Who Are the Older Adults in Your Church, Synagogue, and Community?

We can easily identify seven kinds of older adults in our churches, synagogues, and communities: *active/healthy, inactive/healthy, transitionally impaired, homebound, frail/feeble, institutionalized, and dying.*

The *active/healthy* status are older adults who are on the go. They are the ones who are actively involved in the life of the church or synagogue and the community. Active/healthy older adults are teaching in the church/synagogue school, serving on church/synagogue committees, singing in the choir, learning in classes, or providing other beneficial services to the church/synagogue. They may be involved in civic organizations or engaged in political activities. One word can easily describe their lifestyle: busy.

Churches, synagogues, and communities are filled with active/healthy older adults. We see them on the streets, pass them in the stores, sit with them in the pews. They are the people who demonstrate successful aging to persons of all ages.

Inactive/healthy older adults are persons who have succumbed to the myths and stereotyping of older adulthood. They have found their rocking chair, and they are sitting in it! Their health is good, but they live a cloistered life: going nowhere and doing nothing, except perhaps waiting to die. They are often the ones who say, "I did my part, now it's up to the younger people to take over." Inactive/healthy older adults are not motivated to engage the world or their faith in a meaningful way.

Older adults who are *transitionally impaired* are at a particularly crucial point in their life. They may be in a transitional stage due to a sudden illness or great loss. Perhaps they have recently suffered a stroke or heart attack, or experienced the unexpected death of a spouse. They find their lives in transition, one which they did not choose but happened nevertheless.

It is said that "time heals all wounds"; however, a caring community can help older adults who are transitionally impaired regain their active/healthy lifestyle. This may be more difficult if the cause of the transition is a major medical problem. If this is the case, or there is no supportive, caring community, a transitionally impaired person may become an inactive/healthy older adult or homebound.

Homebound older adults are usually thought of as persons who are physically unable to be actively involved in the life of the church/synagogue or community. Often they are persons who would like to participate more in the life of the faith community, but for health or caregiving reasons are unable to do so. Some are homebound out of fear for their safety or due to a lack of social services, including transportation. Occasionally the church or synagogue may make a special effort to involve these persons in the life of the faith community.

Persons who are homebound may keep abreast of the activities and concerns facing the local congregation or community. Many can and want to be involved in ministry. The faith community must find ways of inviting their participation and engaging them in continued spiritual growth.

The *frail/feeble* older adults are usually the oldest group of older adults. They may have experienced one or more serious chronic debilitating conditions that impede their normal functioning as an adult. As a result of poor health conditions, frail/feeble older adults may be unable to participate at any time in the life of the faith community. This does not mean that the faith community can ignore its responsibility to such persons. They need the ministries of the faith community—especially the rites and rituals offered and nurturing through our presence. Also, the frail/feeble in our faith communities have something to teach us. The frail/feeble elderly can help us understand what it means to be dependent upon God.

About five percent of older adults live in institutions such as nursing homes. *Institutionalized* older adults may be any of the following: active/healthy, inactive/healthy, transitionally impaired, frail, or dying. As people grow older, their chances of becoming residents in nursing homes or continuing care facilities increases. Many older adults may spend at least some time in an institutional setting. Following surgery or hospitalization, some older adults need the assistance of quality nursing care until they are well enough to return to their homes.

The *dying* are with us at every age, but primarily they are with us when they are old. What do the dying have to teach us? How can the church/synagogue be engaged in an intentional ministry with the dying? How can the faith community care for the caregivers of the dying?

As we look at the growing aging population, the challenge of church and synagogue to minister to all of these becomes apparent.

Some Myths Associated with Aging and Older Adults

Myths about aging are usually the result of stereotyping. According to gerontologist Georgia Barrow, "Stereotypes are generalized beliefs or opinions produced by irrational thinking."[15] But they can also be generalizations based on one's own limited understanding and experiences. Although stereotypes are irrational and limiting, such beliefs are reinforced in society, especially by the media.

Since stereotypes do not take into account individual differences, they fail to give us a true picture of aging and older adults. As a result, stereotyping of older adults often leads to ageism.[16] "At best a stereotype conveys only partial information, and more often it conflicts with lived experience, communicating a particular set of beliefs, an ideological view, about the group."[17]

Ageist generalizations made about older adults often dwell on decline of mental faculties, lifestyle, and health conditions. In order to ensure a reasonable place for older adults in our congregations and within society, the influence of ageism must be dispelled. Let us look at three commonly held myths associated with aging and older adults.

Myth 1: As people grow older, their ability to learn decreases.

In this age of rapid change and knowledge explosion, it is a tremendous challenge for persons at any age to stay informed. However, the ability to learn for older adults does not decrease simply because of chronological age. If given sufficient time, understanding, and circumstances, most older adults can learn as well as younger persons.

Hearing and vision loss and other physical or biological changes may impede or change the way an older adult learns; however, old age can be a time of continual learning. Paul Maves declares, "For a long time there has been a cliché that one cannot teach new tricks to an old dog. But older people can and do learn. There are those among us who are learning new languages, learning to type or to use computers and calculators, mastering new games, learning to play musical instruments, and acquiring new artistic skills. Some of us are enrolling in college classes and securing degrees. We are taking up painting and weaving. We are reading and attending lectures to keep us abreast of current events."[18]

Myth 2: Older adults want to disengage from life.

A common view of aging in our society is that older adulthood is not a period when growth and purposeful living occurs, but rather, it is more nearly a time to wait for death. Not many years ago, some gerontologists believed that as persons grew older, they should gradually withdraw from all social networks. At the same time, society was encouraged to lower expectations of aging persons and to reduce interaction with them.

There is little empirical evidence to support this notion of a mutual separation of the older person from society. More often, this view of aging has been used to reinforce mistaken and prejudicial assumptions about the needs of the older population.

In time, gerontologists came to understand older adults not simply as deteriorating organisms waiting for total fading from the human scene. Instead, they began to understand that older adults continue to live in relation to others, use God-given talents and abilities, and grow and experience a meaningful life.

Successful aging today involves selective engagement and disengagement from life's activities. The proper amount of activity depends upon the individual. The important point is that older adults, no less than other persons, should have the right to choose the direction and the scope of their involvement in a meaningful life.

Myth 3: Older adults are in poor health

The majority of older adults in their early retirement years are relatively healthy and are not as limited in activity as frequently assumed—even if they have chronic illnesses. While health and mobility do decline with advancing age, as a result of better nutrition, health care, medical technology, and working conditions, people are living better and healthier today than ever before.

As indicated earlier in this chapter, a majority of older adults describe their health as excellent, very good, or good. While older persons may experience multiple chronic conditions, most older adults believe they are in good health and actually do feel healthy.

Although recent surveys exclude the institutionalized older adult population in identifying health conditions, the results are a good indicator of the overall health status of the elderly in our communities.

Before reading chapter 2, you may want to take an inventory of your knowledge about aging and older adults. (See *Facts on Aging: Quiz,* Appendix C, and *Facts on Aging: Answers*, Appendix D.) This inventory is also useful for training seminars and workshops for leaders of older adult ministries.

Chapter 2

SPIRITUAL
NEEDS OF
OLDER ADULTS

W hile much has been written in the past decade or two about aging and older adults, most studies and resources have addressed the economic, social, psychological, and physical aspects of aging. One area that is beginning to receive a lot of attention is the spiritual needs of older adults.

Our spirituality encompasses all that we are and do. It is living with the ordinary and commonplace things in life, and being open and ready to find God there. Such living elicits trust, awe, and wonder in each of us. It brings us to a sense of faithfulness that can be described as "transformational," or better still, "turning one's heart toward God."

The National Interfaith Coalition on Aging (NICA) spent much time in the decade of the seventies surveying ministries with and for older adults from participating religious bodies under a project funded by the Administration on Aging and entitled, "A Survey of Aging Programs Under Religious Auspices." The study produced a one-sentence definition of spiritual well-being that has guided

NICA's work: **Spiritual well-being is the affirmation of life in a relationship with God, self, community, and environment that nurtures and celebrates wholeness**. Without an emphasis on spiritual well-being, older adults are made to feel useless, ashamed of their age, alienated for being unproductive, and devoid of purpose.[1]

The F.A.C.E.S. of Aging

One way of addressing the spiritual needs of older adults is to identify the many F.A.C.E.S. of aging. These are the worn and wrinkled faces of the years, the joyful faces of dreams fulfilled and loves shared, and the sorrowful faces of defeat and failure that time may bring. These faces (or F.A.C.E.S., which identifies the first letter of each spiritual need) can easily be seen as we look at the following spiritual needs of older adults.

1. Finding worth in one's being, not through having or doing.

Our society places great emphasis on the productivity of people. We measure our worth by the amount of money we make, the home and place where we live, the car we drive, and the educational and occupational status we have achieved.

In a society that devalues the importance of religion, it isn't easy for us to see our worth solely as children of God. We fail to remember the words of Isaiah:

> *Listen to me, O house of Jacob ... even to your old age I am he; even when you turn gray I will carry you. I have made, and I will bear; I will carry and will save.*
>
> (Isaiah 46:3a-4).

Our worth is not in the amount of money we have amassed or the social status we have achieved, but in our relationship to God and humanity. Our oneness with God is that we are loved by God not for *who* we are, but for *whose* we are. As a result, we are able to love others. We cannot attain this relationship with God through anything less than humble submission to the mere fact that what we have and what we have done is God's.

2. Accepting one's life journey and faith story.

Albert Camus once wrote, "There is but only one truly serious problem, and that is . . . judging whether life is or is not worth living."[2] Erik Erickson defined the last crisis of adulthood as *Ego Integrity vs. Despair*.[3] Erickson believed that this last crisis provided older adults the opportunity to sort out whether their life has had meaning or is filled with regrets. He suggested that old age is a time when persons look back on life and answer the question, "Is growing old worth one's whole life to attain?"

Faith experiences begin early and continue throughout all of life. They tell of struggles and new beginnings, of a relationship between God and the believer that is gathered up in a story, our story of a faith journey.

Life review and reminiscence are useful tools for older adults to reflect on, claim, and accept one's life journey and faith story. They do this silently, when they sit quietly and remember days long ago. They do this publicly when they are given the opportunity to tell others their stories about the past.

Remembering can be a traumatic and emotional experience. It may cause tears and fears. But by being engaged in remembering their life, older adults are able to work through the answer to their deepest question and discover that life has meaning through our loving and being loved.

3. Confronting losses and acknowledging our gains.

There are losses associated with aging. Some of these losses include:

- *The loss of significant loved ones.* This may be the death of a spouse or parents, a child, siblings, friend, or pet. It may be that children and grandchildren are moving across country and close physical contact is greatly diminished. It is never easy to say "good-bye" to someone we love. Experiencing the death of a relationship can have a profound and lasting impact on the life of older adults.

- *The loss of aspects of self.* As we grow old, the biological effects of aging take their toll: decreased energy, muscle tone, and hearing. Hair becomes silver or gray, thinning or balding, while there is a decrease in one's ability to smell, taste, or see clearly. Chronic illnesses increase and the generally good health we once enjoyed begins to wane.

- *The loss of external objects.* When persons retire, there is a loss or lowering of income which impacts a variety of material losses. If we are no longer able to live alone or maintain the house we live in, we may find it necessary to make other living arrangements, thus giving up our home of many years. If our physical condition is such that it becomes necessary to give up our driver's license, we no longer drive the automobile that transported us to and from work, the store, the church or synagogue, or the visiting with family and friends.

- *The loss of time.* Young adults measure time since birth; older adults measure time until death. Time may be seen as the enemy. On one hand, there is time to do things one could not do during the childrearing and working years (see the discussion of gains associated with aging below); on the other hand, time is running out. Aunt Irene had always wanted to visit Israel, but with advancing old age, decreasing physical condition, and loss of income, she saw time running out on achieving her dream.

- *The loss of independence.* As persons age, there is greater likelihood that they will need to rely more and more on the help of others. With increasing health care, there may be need for assistance in activities of daily living. Older adults become more dependent upon gadgets, aids, and other people.

- *The loss of purpose.* All persons need to be accepted, respected, needed, and loved. For older adults, this is a time when questions of life's purpose begin to surface. When people are younger, their purpose is often measured by the work they do. This may be in the nurturing of a family or the occupation they have attained. Without a family to nurture or work to be fulfilled, older adults may experience a loss of purpose. This loss is deeply ingrained in one's spirituality and must be resolved for spiritual well-being to be achieved.

In ministry, it is impossible for us to ignore the impact losses make upon the lives of older adults. Confronting losses can play a major role in helping older adults make sense out of their lives and find purpose and meaning in living.

In addition to confronting our losses as we grow older, there is also another important aspect of aging–and that is acknowledging our gains. Society often sees only the losses associated with aging, never the gains. Aging is a gift from God. It is not a disease, unnatural, or morbid. Aging is a process involving the whole life span from conception and birth to death. It provides us with many opportunities for continued growth even in old age. Some of these gains include:

- *Discovering helpful adult dependencies.* Wearing eyeglasses or a hearing aid may seem like a nuisance when we misplace our glasses or use our hearing aid in a noisy, crowded room, but what useful devices they are to enable us to see and hear more clearly. Likewise, relying on others, knowing that we are interdependent with one another, is a valuable insight to be gained. While we might become more dependent upon gadgets, aids, and other people, we are able to live life fully and with meaning as we learn to acknowledge and accept helpful adult dependencies.

- *Relaxing one's defenses.* When we are young, we have a tendency to be defensive about who we are, what we have achieved, and what we are doing with our lives. As we grow older, we can relax our defenses. We know that acquiring material things and achieving social status is not important. What is important is our oneness with God and humanity. We don't have to be defensive because we have come to realize that we are a child of God and that God loves us even with all our weaknesses and failings.

- *Redefining one's status.* Over the years, our status has been wrapped in what we do or perhaps who we were married to. As we age, we have an opportunity to redefine our status. Again, our status is not wrapped up in any of these things. They do not matter. But our status as a child of God gives us the advantage of reaching out and growing in new ways.

• *Creating new work opportunities.* Being retired from the rigors of the everyday world of work offers older adults the opportunity to seek out new experiences. This may involve a part-time job or a whole new career. It may be volunteer or paid opportunities. It may be finding hidden talents that long lay dormant, or discovering new talents one never knew existed. Many older adults have found new opportunities to be leaders, painters, writers, or other creative entrepreneurs by looking inside themselves and seeing the needs of others and adapting or learning new skills to meet these needs.

• *Providing time for spiritual growth.* Marking time for older adults may seem like a loss because there is so little time left, but the time that does remain offers older adults the opportunity to grow in their spiritual faith. When persons are younger and involved in life's many daily activities, such as childrearing and working on the job, there never seems to be enough time for spiritual growth and a deepening relationship with God. As we age, without childrearing responsibilities or a full-time occupation, we have more time to spend in prayer, meditation, Torah or Bible reading, and other activities that provide nourishment for our souls.

4. Experiencing a new (or renewed) relationship with God.
As stated above in the gains associated with aging, spiritual nurture and growth is important for older adults. Spiritual growth, like learning, is a continuous process. Deepening our relationship with God is an important spiritual need of older adults.
Throughout life, the normal person constantly finds himself or herself facing situations that require adjustment, rethinking, new attitudes, new and different actions. So it is with old age.

Nicodemus asked Jesus, "How can anyone be born after having grown old?" (John 3:4). We might ask a similar question today, "Is it possible for us to grow in our faith now that we are old?" Just as Jesus encouraged Nicodemus, so we are encouraged to experience a new or renewed relationship with God. Spiritual growth is possible and important for older adults. Just because a person is an older adult does not mean that he or she ceases to grow in faith.

Just because one is old does not mean that she or he has all the faith one needs.

We all need to grow in faith and in our relationship with God in order that we are better able to face the dilemmas and challenges of life. Without a growing faith, we lack the resource of One who can give life meaning and hope in times of fear, loss, and uncertainty.

5. Serving the needs of others.

As we stated earlier, spiritual well-being is not something lived in isolation, but lived in relation to God, self, community, and environment. Ministering to the needs of others helps make life worth living and gives importance to older adults. Time, knowledge, and experience can go a long way in helping meet the needs of others. Providing caregiving services, tutoring children, teaching church or synagogue school, going on a short- or long-term work mission, and sharing one's faith journey with the faith community are just some of the many ways older adults can help others.

Older adults need to know and to feel themselves spiritually integrated to God, self, others, and creation. Spiritual well-being for older adults includes: (1) a commitment to the great causes of justice, peace, and environmental protection; (2) a deeper bond of love and service for God and fellow human beings; and (3) a new interior growth of spiritual life through faith, hope, and love.

Through such an approach older adults will not only self-actualize but they will transcend themselves for greater causes. This self-transcendence will lead them out of their ego-centered existence and help them to do something for the generations to come, that nature may be preserved, that justice may triumph, that the oppression of sexism, racism, (ageism), and ethnocentrism may end, and that people may love each other and God.[4]

Wisdom Associated with Older Adults

When we lived primarily in an agrarian society, wisdom could be gained by the amount of seasons one had experienced. Older adults were knowledgeable in knowing when to till, plant, and harvest. Wisdom was not something people received just because they had read volumes of books or participated in higher education and learning. Wisdom, which could be possessed by the learned and unlearned alike, was knowledge gained over time. The longer a person lived, the greater the opportunity to obtain wisdom.

Today, living in an increasingly changing world, where advances in technology and new information are constantly before us, are older adults seen as having wisdom? In an age when children and grandchildren are more knowledgeable about computers and telecommunications than their parents and grandparents, where is the wisdom which older persons should have?

The Bible suggests that wisdom is associated with older adults: "Wisdom is with the aged, and understanding in length of days" (Job 12:12, RSV). Wisdom is not a capacity to solve all human problems, or even to understand them fully. But over time, through the many and various experiences of life, older adults can have an ability to view problems, to appreciate them, and to see them in their wholeness. Experience provides us with important information which enables us in future decision-making.

Unfortunately, in many congregations older adults are not viewed as "wisdom people." In her book, *The Coming of Age*, Simone de Beauvoir tells the story about a legend in a mountainous region of Bali.

> *In Bali it is said that once upon a time the people of a remote mountain village used to sacrifice and eat their old men. A day came when there was not a single old man left, and the traditions were lost. They wanted to build a great house for the meetings of the assembly, but when they came to look at the tree-trunks that had been cut for that purpose no one could tell the top from the bottom: if the timber were placed the wrong way up, it would set off a series of disasters. A young man said that if they promised never to eat the old men any more, he would be able to find a solution. They promised. He brought his grandfather, whom he had hidden; and the old man taught the community to tell top from bottom.*[5]

While we may not sacrifice and eat old men, we must be careful that the wealth of wisdom, experience, and faith which often abound in older adults is not lost or under-utilized.

Older adults have experienced the realities of life and have persevered. They are survivors. As a great natural resource, they hold the keys to the future of our congregations.

It has been said that the future of the church/synagogue is in its children and youth. We believe the future of the church/synagogue is in the hands of its older adults. We believe this is true for several reasons:

1. Many churches and synagogues are filled with older adults.

Perhaps most congregations have a high proportion of older adults in their memberships. Older adults participate in the life of the faith community through worship, study, and service.

2. Many of the teachers, rabbis, ministers/pastors, priests, and other leaders in congregations are older adults.

They are the ones engaged in teaching and learning, in maintaining or changing policies, in helping to conform or transform congregational life.

3. Older adults give financially to the church/synagogue.

Often, older adults are the most generous givers in their faith community. Loren Mead points out that "all of the evidence we have points in one direction: Younger generations do not contribute to religious institutions as generously as did their elders."[6] This is probably related to different understandings of stewardship and to age-cohort effects.

Nevertheless, battles are waged in many congregations between young adults and older adults about how money is spent. For older adults, who were raised during the depression, saving money is important. For younger generations, raised with a different understanding about financial matters, they may want to spend. Since the proportion of giving dollars is higher among older adults than younger adults, older adults may be more cautious about spending because they realize that they may indeed have to pay for it.

4. Older adults have the time to give to service.

While younger women and men may be engaged in raising a family or building a career, older adults have the time to serve the needs of their congregation and community. Many older adults provide necessary and vital service as volunteers in hospitals and community services.

Older adults, as they grow in years, have a wonderful opportunity to deepen their relationship with God. They have the time, and often the longing, to nurture a closer relationship with the One who is Creator and Sustainer of all life. Torah or Bible study, worship, and prayer are key ingredients to their closer walk with God.

But it doesn't end there. Older adults need to connect fully with themselves, other people, and the rest of creation. When they do, they can be persons of great insight and understanding. They can indeed be the "wisdom people" for any day and age. As Mordecai said to Queen Esther, "Who knows? Perhaps you have come to royal dignity for just such a time as this" (Esther 4:14).

Chapter 3

THEOLOGY
OF AGING

The church and synagogue have a significant responsibility to aging persons for several reasons:

1. The great majority of older adults identify with the church and synagogue and look to their religious faith as a source of strength and hope.

2. Older adults in their retirement years as the "third age: the new generation"[1] want guidance to seek their full potential as "seasoned citizens" in their "creative leisure" and "elective years."

3. Older adults turn to their religious faith to find the ultimate meaning of life.

4. Older adults seek to be enabled by their religious faith to use their wisdom and experience in facing the depth issues of society.

5. Older adults are children of God and as such need a theology of aging that emphasizes the rich value and significance they have to God and to their fellow human beings.

The stirring challenge to develop a theology of aging which would undergird an effective and meaningful ministry *with* aging persons is not a call peculiar to our age and time. The long line of the Judeo-Christian heritage and tradition has for thousands of years called clergy and lay leaders in synagogue and church:

- *To nourish the spirit, mind, and body of older persons with sensitivity for the dignity and wholeness of each individual before God*

- *To open doors for living and giving to older people, with a theology that is vital and meaningful for the aging.*

Therefore, it is well for us to look at the Jewish and Christian views of old age which become the basis for a meaningful theology of aging.

A Jewish View of Old Age

Robert Katz of Hebrew Union College-Jewish Institute of Religion, as recorded in Seward Hiltner's *Toward a Theology of Aging*,[2] has set forth views on aging coming from the Jewish tradition. He speaks from a rich knowledge of the Jewish religion and tradition and applies this knowledge to contemporary reflection on the condition of aging persons in at least three ways.

Aging in Jewish literature
According to Katz, aging in many Jewish sources is presented as a valued status, one with privileges denied to others. A man or woman can be venerable without being old, while others live long without achieving character. For the rabbis in Jewish tradition, the ideal state was to attain both old age and honor.

Well known are the statements in the Scriptures mandating respect for the aged. In Leviticus 19:32, we read, "You shall rise before the aged, and defer to the old . . ." According to Proverbs 16:31, "Gray hair is a crown of glory; it is gained in a righteous life."

Job 12:12 raises the question, "Is wisdom with the aged, and understanding in length of days?" But there is no answer. However, in the Mishnah, note is taken of the fact that a new jar can be full of old wine (wisdom) and an old one may not even contain new wine (4:20), but elsewhere in the context, Katz says we are informed that learning from the aged is like drinking old wine. A Talmudic source goes so far as to maintain that as the older scholars grow, the greater their wisdom becomes.

Aging and social class (justice and equality)

Katz shares an insight that one of the most important phenomenon of aging is class status. We can easily become involved in generalizing about older persons and their needs on the basis of the social class(es) with which we are most familiar. When, for example, we speak of "disengagement from the work force" or use the term "role exit," we are really thinking of the working middle-class who may radically change their lifestyle when they attain the age of retirement. The lower-class people may never be able to retire or "disengage from the work force."

Upper-class members whose income has been derived from ownership of property or stocks and bonds do not make a "role exit." The rich lose no self-esteem; are not rejected; are not abandoned by their family, friends, and community; are not likely to be consigned by their families to nursing homes; do not live in fear of the erosion of their pensions or Social Security; and are not set adrift by their families. Such experiences are reserved only for the middle and lower classes. Wealth does not command immortality, but it normally discourages disrespect and neglect.

This brings up the theological issue of justice and equality for *all* of God's children. The development of a new ideology of aging which recognizes the equal status of all older adults before God and the renewal of our commitment to a society of justice and equality is a theological imperative.

Aging, the "Sabbath" of human life

In the Jewish view, men and women are not only encouraged but obliged to hope for a Messianic Age. In the vision of the end of days, a time of peace and love, the aged, too, will attain happiness and enjoy the highest esteem, for they represent human beings in their state of highest self-fulfillment as children of God.

Life becomes an unending Sabbath for the individual reaching the years of maturity; it persists for that person until the day of death. According to Katz, nothing captures the essence of a theology of aging in Judaism as does the concept of aging as the Sabbath of the soul with its rich possibilities for self-realization.

In the Messianic thought of Judaism, the individual who attains old age is not to be degraded, but to be honored. The aged can now address themselves to high purposes such as the study of God's Word and the purification and refinement of the soul.

As the Sabbath was in Genesis of the Hebrew Scriptures the climax of creation, so the time of maturity represents the highest point of human development—a time for rest, but more to "refresh oneself." To be refreshed in the Jewish tradition refers to activity that is creative and vibrant and yields a sense of renewal and inspiration.

Judaism is a magnificent defense of leisure. In the language of the rabbis, Judaism sanctifies time. You do not "kill" time or "pass" time to fill the void in retirement. In the Sabbath concept you use it for study, prayer, and contemplation.

Rabbi Richard F. Address, director of the Committee on Older Adults of the Union of American Hebrew Congregations (UAHC), has shared his viewpoint of the Jewish theology of aging in the context of a letter he wrote to congregational leaders of his faith. This letter appeared as an introduction to the 1995 manual, *Preparing for the Graying of a Congregation*, compiled and published by the UAHC Committee on Older Adults.[3]

Within this letter, Rabbi Address makes these statements:

> *Congratulations on your desire to reach out in meaningful and exciting ways to the older adult population of your congregation. As you may be aware, this aspect of our congregational community is undergoing changes that are challenging and instructive to the entire community.*
>
> *Demographers now tell us that by the year 2000 almost one fifth of the Jewish population will be over 65, with the greatest percentage increase in*

those "old, old" over 75. Those same demographers also tell us that as the number of individuals over 75 increases ... to include even greater numbers living into their eighties and nineties, it will not be uncommon to see this older adult "third stage" of life potentially including some three decades of time. This is not the same old "senior citizens" club!

*As a synagogue community, it is important for us to remember, as we begin to respond to this new older adult population, that what we do teaches a lesson and sets an example. In developing responses to and working with your congregation's population of older adults and their families, **it is important to keep in mind the ever growing and essential search for personal meaning and the "holy".**[4] Increasingly, researchers are confirming that many within our synagogue community have been slowly experiencing the rekindling of the search for Judaism's truths as they relate to older adults. Older adults issues go to the heart of how we decide what is blessing and what is not. We need that torah, that instruction. Indeed, for the Jew, healthy aging means a healthy understanding of what Jewish faith, tradition, values and ethics have to say about where on life's journey one might be ...*

Thus, as we age, the value of our experiences increases and the desire to see our existence in the context of overall meaningful and transcendence becomes ever more powerful. The opportunities for mitzvot (deeds of loving kindness), holiness and caring are key to what we do as a synagogue community. Indeed, it is what sets us apart.

...The coming generation of older adults will be vitally interested in their personal quest for meaning and purpose. They will seek religious institu-

tions which challenge them spiritually as well as intellectually.

As you develop your programs (enhancing the life of older adults), it is necessary to remember that each individual is connected to family and friends, and that often, given our high propensity for mobility, an older adult's support network may not be close at hand. Caregiving, both local and long distance, is an increasingly important source of concern and offers exciting and challenging possibilities for involvement. Care for the caregivers is a mitzvah that needs to be addressed as part of an overall response to the needs of individuals and families ...

As you set to work with your congregational family,[5] remember that we do a disservice to people when we stereotype them. Judaism teaches that we are unique individuals, each choosing our own special way of leading life's journey. Growing older is as individual as the person before us. Just as each person has lived differently, each person will age differently. This call to tear down age-based stereotypes and elevate attitudes that honor each person as an individual, no matter what age, is reflected in a classic essay by Abraham Joshua Heschel entitled, To Grow in Wisdom.

Heschel writes:"We must seek ways to overcome the traumatic fear of being old, prejudice, discrimination against those advance years. Being old is not necessarily the same as being stale. The effort to restore dignity of old age will depend upon our ability to revive the equation of old age and wisdom. Wisdom is the substance upon which the inner security of the old will forever depend. But the attainment of wisdom is the work of a lifetime."

*Honoring that work and celebrating that wisdom
is at the heart of what we must be as a family of
congregations and as congregation families.
The Midrash tells us that some people live for years
and remain vital, while others, despite relative
youth, are quicker to lose that sense of vitality. As
our older adult population swells, reflecting
increasingly diverse populations and life experiences, it is well to remember that at the heart of
everything we do there are unique human
beings–images of God–with hopes and dreams,
wishes and fears, family and friends ... Our congregational community continues to have as a basic
mission the responsibility to look at who we are
and thus respond to the present and future needs
of our members (including older adults). In that
way do we set the example of a mitzvah-driven
caring community.*[6]

Rabbi Address summarizes his Jewish theology of aging in a
statement on theological foundation from the Union of American
Hebrew Congregations Committee on Older Adults. It is as follows:

*At the heart of Judaism's understanding of aging
and the older adult is a fundamental ethic that
speaks to the dignity and sanctity of human life.
Drawn from our understanding that we are created "b'tzelem elohim" (in the image and likeness of
God), Judaism understands that each and every
human being is distinguished by this "covenantal"
relationship, empowered with the freedom to
choose one's path along life's journey.*

*It is within that framework that Judaism embraces
growing older not as a period of decline and
diminished capacity, but as that natural part of life
that, if properly understood and embraced, allows
for ever more meaningful personal and spiritual*

growth. This openness to life and life's potential is key to Judaism. Constantly we are reminded that this "covenantal" partnership is the theological foundation for our view of life; a life that implores the Jew to constantly seek ways of sanctifying life by doing "mitzvot" (deeds of loving kindness). All of this can be drawn from our understanding of the basic text in Genesis of being created in God's image."[7]

This life-oriented view allows us to see aging as part of the natural order of creation, part of our relationship with God. Note Leviticus 19:32: "You shall rise before the aged and show deference to the old; you shall fear your God: I am the Lord." Growing older in Jewish life and thought emphasizes growing. All of us, as part of our human condition, become older. In a sacred relationship with God, one that dignifies and sanctifies life, we may continue to grow. This synthesis of God and life and our own experience form a theological foundation upon which Judaism creates its view of aging.[8]

A Christian View of Aging

Christian theology has been described as philosophical reflection upon our common human experience and language and upon Christian tradition (i.e., the significant texts, symbols, gestures, and personal witnesses of the Christian history). With this definition in mind, the following theological concepts on aging have real meaning.

Aging, the fulfillment of life

Henri Nouwen and Walter Gaffney, in their book *Aging, The Fulfillment of Life*, have shared this penetrating, universal concept which touches *all* persons. They illuminate their theological basis for understanding aging by defining aging as *"the gradual fulfillment of the life cycle in which receiving matures in giving and living makes dying worthwhile."*[9]

When aging can be experienced as growing by giving, not only of mind and heart, but of life itself, then it can become a movement towards the hour when we say with the Apostle Paul writing in Timothy 4:6-7: "As for me, I am already being poured out as a libation, and the time of my departure has come. I have fought the good fight, I have finished the race, I have kept the faith."

Nouwen and Gaffney believe that aging is an experience that is so profoundly human that it breaks through the artificial boundaries between childhood and adulthood, and between adulthood and old age with a rainbow of promises. It can move from the darkness of pessimism into the way of light and hope. For example, an aged person like Simeon (Luke 2:25-32) can break through all pessimism and reveal new visions, new sounds, and new light for life. Aging can be growing into the light in such a way that as we age, we see new visions, hear new sounds, and find new directions for living in service to God and to our fellow human beings. Jesus called this being "lights of the world and the salt of the earth" (Matthew 5:13-16).

Thus, aging is so filled with promises that it can lead us to discover more and more of life's treasures. Aging is not a reason for despair, but a basis of hope; not a slow decaying, but a gradual maturing; not a fate to be undergone, but a change to be embraced.[10]

Aging is the fulfillment in life which God revealed through God's Son, Jesus. When Jesus, the Christ, was nailed to the cross, robbed of all human dignity, he knew that he had reached the fulfillment of age even at thirty to thirty-three years and said: "It is finished" (John 19:30). The death and resurrection of Jesus has become the sign of continual hope and new life for many who seek the light in their aging lives. Jesus was the light that came into the darkness, and revealed to us that the life cycle of aging is not a return to second childhood, but one step *forward* in the journey of our salvation.

Nouwen and Gaffney remind us that *every* human being has only one life cycle to live, but together our aging can become the fulfillment of the promise of him who by his life, aging, and death brought new life to the world. Every man and woman who has discovered the deep meaning of his or her own aging, therefore, has a unique opportunity to enrich the quality of his or her own life by sharing the experience of aging as a fulfillment of life with others.

Aging, a pilgrimage from birth to life

Reuel Howe in his book, *Live All Your Life!*, lifts up the theme, "The Pilgrimage from Birth to Life."[11] He speaks of the great relevance of aging during *all* stages of life. Our willingness *to share*, and *to risk* moving forward as God's pilgrims are critical behaviors that decide whether growth and life are to be fostered and maintained. If we grow as persons, we must consciously decide to grow. Growth requires that we risk what we are for the sake of what we would like to be, without any guarantee that we will succeed in finding it. As we grow older, it becomes harder to risk than when we were younger.

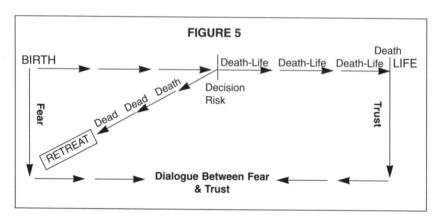

FIGURE 5

Howe illustrates this theology of aging with a diagram. (See Figure 5.) On the left is the pull of fear; on the right, the pull of trust; in the middle between fear and trust is the question as to whether we will risk growth. Fear causes us to turn our backs on growth and life and walk away from it, looking for a place of security. Fearful persons may either become rigid, dogmatic or bigoted; or afraid to hold any convictions and are easily swayed by stronger persons. On the fear side are the words "death and dead," which indicate that because this person has moved away from life in response to fear, he or she is dying or dead.

The opposite of fear is trust and life. Trust pulls us forward, whereas fear pulls us back. Trust-life includes trust in oneself, in others and trust in the healing and reuniting forces in life itself which gives us strength to fight against, if not overcome, the demonic that dwells in us and others.

Note that on the trust-life side, there is mention of death-life. It is inevitable, according to Howe, that there will be a succession of death-life/death-life sequences in the course of our living. Each new and deepened stage of life in the aging life cycle brings us new temptations, challenges, and conflicts. As we have these successes in death-life/death-life experiences, we discover that our trust grows and our confidence and sense of security increases.

Therefore, a theological interpretation of the diagram says that the left side (fear-death) illustrates the truth of what Jesus said: "Those who find their life [in themselves] will lose it." The trust-life side of the diagram represents the other truth, "Those who lose their life for my sake will find it" (Matthew 10:39). This explains in human terms the Christian death-resurrection rhythm of life as lived in response to fear and trust. We don't really know what is on the other side of life in death, but we trust; and our experiences of trust seem to teach us that death and life go together, and are parts of one process.

Aging, from the evangelical Christian perspective

Frederick C. Van Tatenhove[12] writes on the evangelical Christian perspective of a theology of aging in the 1995 handbook on *Aging, Spirituality and Religion*.[13]

He points out that "aging is a fact of life" and therefore "influences all aspects of life." Aging must be considered in "any attempt to understand the meaning of life."[14]

When one looks at a theology of aging from an "evangelical" perspective, the first aspect which Van Tatenhove lifts up is "the belief that human beings are part of a interrelated, holistic order, created by God. Thus, theological reflections about aging cannot be confined to one area of human existence and experience."[15] Only in recent history has aging been viewed as a human phenomenon which raises critical questions for theology. Yet, such a theology of aging does deserve our attention.

Theological reflection on aging to the "evangelical" is "biblically based and confessionally believed."[16] Central emphasis is placed upon "the biblical teaching that human beings are unique (Genesis 1:27). Each person is created to be in a relationship with God."[17] In fact, all persons *of any age* are included in God's redemptive grace. This understanding was given special attention by the Apostle Paul, who proclaimed Christ as the "Son of God" (Acts 9:20) and called people to live their lives in Christ (Gal. 2:20; Eph. 3:17; Col. 1:27).

The acceptance of aging as a part of the created order means that people are important as a special creation of God and have "a covenantal relationship with God.[18] "People created in the image of God do not diminish in worth or sanctity as they move through the aging process. To be human is to represent God. Therefore, the image of God is not something people achieve or something people do. Rather, it is what one is to be in God's intended plan."[19]

To a Christian, the teachings of Jesus suggest the best response to the aging process—and this is to seek fullness of life at every stage of our existence. To desire to be "the people of God" no matter how old we are is to enable any person to experience what Jesus implies in his words, "I came that they may have life, and have it abundantly" (John 10:10).[20]

Therefore, in summary, God through God's Son, Jesus Christ, calls *all people* in *every stage of life* to be in a redemptive, dynamic relationship with Himself. "This relationship shapes life and influences all other relationships. The worth and sanctity of each individual is intrinsic to being formed in the image of God. Aging does not diminish the gift of God's redemptive grace given to those who 'hunger and thirst for righteousness' (Matt. 5:6). When this truth is central, a biblical understanding of aging is possible."[21]

With the witness of all these theological/biblical concepts of ministry and aging coming from our Judeo-Christian heritage, men and women, clergy and lay leaders of the church and synagogue are called to the challenge of involvement in a significant ministry *with* the aging.

Chapter 4

GETTING STARTED
IN OLDER ADULT
MINISTRIES

If, as we have seen in chapter 1, the population of older persons is increasing in our society and faith communities, the church and synagogue have a responsibility for providing an intentional ministry with older adults.

Abraham was seventy-five years of age when God called him to leave his home and to take his family where God would lead him (Genesis 12:4). Moses was eighty years of age when God called him in a burning bush that was not consumed to lead God's people out of bondage and slavery in Egypt (Exodus 7:7). God is now calling older adults to be in ministry in our society and the world.

If churches and synagogues are intentional about utilizing this vast resource of older adults, how do they get started? Where do they begin? What are they to be about doing? In this chapter we will take a look at how we can intentionally develop older adult ministries.

The Primary Task of the Local Church/Synagogue

Designing an intentional ministry with older adults is an essential ingredient in helping laity live out the primary task of the local congregation and synagogue. If you are asked, "What is the primary task of your local church or synagogue?" how would you answer? Some might answer that the primary task is "saving souls," or "glorifying God," or "meeting the social and spiritual needs of the people in the community," or other insightful response.

We believe the primary task for the local church/synagogue is **faith development.** By this we mean that the primary task, mission, or purpose of the local church or synagogue is **helping people become disciples.** This is a central pronouncement of the Torah (Deuteronomy 6:4-5) and that of the teachings of Jesus (Mark 12:29-30), calling upon us to grow in our faith until we "love the Lord our God with all our heart, and with all our soul, and with all our mind, and with all our strength and our neighbor as ourselves."

In other words, the task of congregations is to help members identify their call, nurture them in faith, and send them out into the world as disciples.[1]

How is the primary task lived out in the life of the local church or synagogue? There are four ingredients:

- Reaching out into the community and receiving all people into the faith family.
- Encouraging people in their relationship to God.
- Providing opportunities for them to be nurtured and to practice the disciplines of their faith.
- Supporting, equipping, and sending them out to live and act as faithful children in covenant with their God for service in the world.

The following information in this chapter will be especially useful for your church or synagogue in its planning ministry with older adults.

Role of the Coordinator of Older Adult Ministries

As we experience an increased number of older adults in our society and in our churches and synagogues, it is important for every congregation to have a coordinator of older adult ministries. The coordinator is one who will oversee, advocate, and enhance the ministries with older adults.

The task of the coordinator of older adult ministries is to assist the local congregation in its ministry with older adults. The coordinator may be a staff person of the local congregation or the elected chairperson of the Older Adult Council. The following are some important qualities that may enhance one's ability to be an effective local church or synagogue coordinator of older adult ministries:

- An articulate person: someone who can communicate effectively and well with others.
- A caring person: someone who is concerned about the spiritual well-being of older adults.
- A faithful person: someone who is both involved in the life of the local congregation and is growing in her or his religious faith.
- A knowledgeable person: someone who is knowledgeable about the organization of the local church or synagogue, resources available in the church or synagogue and community, and issues facing older adults.

The following responsibilities are guidelines for carrying out the work of the coordinator of older adult ministries in the local church or synagogue. After reviewing this list, you may want to identify other responsibilities that are applicable to your congregation and personal situation. The responsibilities are:

1. To work closely with:
- Your minister/pastor, priest, or rabbi;
- Other staff person(s) assigned to the work of older adult ministries;
- Chairperson of the Official Board (or appropriate body);
- Chairperson of the Education Committee (or appropriate body);
- Chairperson of the Outreach/Social Concerns Committee (or appropriate body);
- Chairperson of the Nurture/Caregiving Committee (or appropriate body).

2. To help articulate the vision and mission of the local church or synagogue to older adults.

3. To help articulate the vision and mission of your older adult ministry.

4. To study the needs of older adults in the local congregation and community.

5. To serve as chairperson and conduct regular meetings of the Older Adult Council.

6. To facilitate and coordinate the work of volunteers.

7. To assist in developing a "Needs and Talents" file for all older adults in the congregation and in designing a system for using the information.

8. To assist in surveying the accessibility of church or synagogue.

9. To keep the needs and concerns of older adults before the Official Board (or appropriate title) and program committees of the local congregation.

10. To work with the Official Board (or appropriate title) and program committees of the local congregation in planning and implementing a unified and comprehensive ministry with older adults.

11. To inform older adults about opportunities for learning, teaching, and serving in the congregation and community.

12. To serve as liaison with appropriate organizations, people, and resources in the local congregation and community.

13. **To review and evaluate programs of the local congregation and community as they relate to older adults.**

14. **To continue personal spiritual development.**

15. **To participate in opportunities for continued professional development.**

16. **To advocate on behalf of the needs of older adults in your congregation and community.**

Many churches/synagogues have persons responsible for children, youth, adult, single adult, and young adult ministries because of their concern for the faith development of these persons. Likewise, due to the increasing numbers of older adults in our communities and churches/synagogues, congregations need to have persons identified with the responsibility for ministry with older adults.

Building a Ministry with Older Adults

The following ten steps are designed to help congregations build a ministry with older adults.

Step 1: Organize an older adult council or committee.

If you have an interest in older adults and hold a staff position or have been appointed or elected to serve as the coordinator for older adult ministries in your local congregation, begin by finding another person who shares your hopes, dreams, and concerns. As the two of you discuss your ideas for ministry, think of other persons who might also share your vision. These might be lay leaders in your congregation, young persons who see they have much in common with older adults, trained professionals who might be active or "recycled," technicians-laborers who are active or "recycled," and older volunteers (see chapter 5). Invite these persons to your meeting. You may also want to contact your minister/pastor, rabbi, priest, or other professional staff for suggested names of interested and knowledgeable persons.

Enlist approximately six to thirteen persons (depending upon the age demographics and membership size of your local congregation) and organize an Older Adult Council (or committee, depending upon your church/synagogue policy). In order to have a well-represented body of older adults, the council should be composed of a cross-section of older women and men (e.g., married, single, divorced, homebound, race, ethnic, physically challenged, and church/synagogue organizations).

One or two younger adults who are concerned about aging issues may also serve on the council, but the majority on an Older Adult Council should be older adults themselves in categories already mentioned. If no coordinator has been appointed, a chairperson should be elected during this initial process.

Additional officers should also be elected as needed (e.g., vice-chairperson, recording and correspondence secretaries, treasurer, and program chairpersons, etc.). It is important to go through the proper church/synagogue channels to establish the legitimacy and authority of the council, as well as to secure necessary financial support. If possible, get a line item for older adult ministries in your church/synagogue budget to help finance your ministry.

The work of the council should include the following:

- Studying the needs of older adults in your congregation. If possible you will also want to reach out into your community.
- Interviewing all the older adult members of the congregation.
- Discovering what older adults in the congregation need, think, feel, believe about the church/synagogue and community.
- Developing programs that meet the needs of the various older adult members of the church/synagogue and community.
- Identifying needed resources and key persons for implementing programs.
- Meeting on a regular basis for assessing needs, providing information from reports, planning programs, evaluating existing and ongoing projects.
- Advocating the need for policies, programs, resources, and financial support to help meet the needs of older adults.
- Learning about issues and concerns related to older adults.
- Informing the minister/pastor, priest or rabbi and governing body of the congregation as to the planning, programming, and financial needs of the council.

If you believe that your local congregation is too small in membership to establish an Older Adult Council, we would encourage you to set up a task force and investigate the number and needs of older adults in your congregation. If you find that you have a large number or percentage of older adults even in your small membership congregation, you may find that an Older Adult Council is warranted.

Another method of ministry for small-membership congregations is to develop an Older Adult Council with leadership from several congregations. Involve interested persons from the same faith or denomination in your community or from congregations of other faiths. Often we can minister more effectively together than by ourselves.

Step 2: Gather information about older adults in your congregation.

As a council, develop a survey instrument for gathering information about the older adults in your congregation. In designing a survey form, obtain the following information: (1) name of older adult, his or her address, telephone number, and other general information, (2) needs and concerns of the older adult, and (3) ways older adults can serve the needs of others. (For a sample "Needs and Talents Survey" form, see Appendix E.)

It is important to know as much about the older adults in your congregation and community as possible. Be thorough in asking the right kinds of questions. After you have developed the survey form, you will want to interview all the older adults in your congregation (and community, if feasible).

Before taking your survey, invite your minister/pastor, priest, or rabbi to send a letter to older adults and to place announcements in the weekly bulletin and/or congregation newsletter explaining the survey instrument and interview process. Invite older adults to receive into their homes a trained council member who will share the questionnaire with them.

Train council members to visit older adults. If additional persons are needed for interviewing older adults, train other church/synagogue members to help with the task. Invite older youth and young adults, as well as other adults, to participate in the interviewing process. Be sure that all information received is kept confidential.

It is advisable that you not take along offering envelopes or information about the financial needs of your congregation. While financial matters of the congregation are real and important, the council may give a wrong impression to the older adults they visit. If it appears that the survey is being used by the council simply as a financial ploy on the part of the congregation, the mission of the council and the needs of older adults may not be addressed.

The interview process may look like this:

- Each interviewer should telephone the person(s) he or she is to visit.

- Establish an appropriate date and time for the visit to take place.

- Upon arriving at the home of the older adult, identify yourself and state the reason for your visit. Remember to be warm and friendly. You are an invited guest in their homes.

- When interviewing, take along two survey questionnaires.

- Give one questionnaire to the older adult being interviewed and keep one for recording information. By providing a questionnaire form to the older adult, the interviewer is establishing openness and showing respect. If there are two or more older adults living in the same home, you may want to interview each separately. (Remember to take along enough survey forms for all persons being interviewed and for recording their responses.)

- Generally it is appropriate for one interviewer to visit the home of an older adult. In certain situations, such as high-crime areas, you may decide it is better for safety reasons to have two persons visit at the same time.

- If an older adult no longer lives in your community but maintains membership in your congregation, you will still want to have a survey form completed.

- If the person lives a great distance from your community, making it impossible for an interviewer from your congregation to obtain the necessary information, try to contact the local congregation in the community in which the older adult now resides. This serves three important functions: (1) You will learn about your congregation and community from a former resident, (2) you will identify ways you can be in ministry with this member and how this older adult may continue to grow and serve in faith, and (3) you may help establish a relationship with the older adult and the faith community in which they now reside.)

Step 3: Review existing church/synagogue programs that already involve older adults.

Review your church/synagogue programs and activities. Identify all the programs and activities that involve older adults (see Appendix F for a sample "Church/Synagogue Program Review" form). The purpose of this step is to become familiar with the programs in your church which already involve older adults. Evaluate the effectiveness of these programs and determine whether the activities are ongoing events. As a council, examine whether any other activities should be continued, modified, or added.

As you review existing church/synagogue programs involving older adults, you will want to evaluate your church/synagogue accessibility (see Appendix G for sample form). There are several areas to identify for accessibility: physical, administrative, and educational.

For example, does your church provide accessible restrooms, wheelchair ramps, and handrails? Do you have large-print hymnals, Bibles, and educational literature? Do you have meeting, study, and worship times which are appropriate for older adults who may have difficulty driving at night? Accessibility may be the key ingredient in having older adults participate actively in the life of your congregation.

Step 4: Survey community social service agencies.

In addition to knowing the needs and talents of older adults and identifying and evaluating existing church/synagogue programs and accessibility, you will find it helpful to become aware of existing programs for older adults in your community (see Appendix H for a list of organizations that might be in your community). Encourage council members to visit all the social service agencies in your community. Your area agency on aging office might also be helpful in providing you with necessary information.

Take a survey of their programs and services (see Appendix I). If a community social service agency is providing a program that meets the needs of older adults, don't try to duplicate or compete. Find out ways your older adults can utilize the service or help with the program.

Ask the social service agencies to identify areas of unmet need. It may be possible that the services not now being rendered could be provided by your congregation.

Step 5: Develop a shared vision.

What do you want to see happen as a result of your older adult ministries? What do you hope to achieve? As a council, you need to articulate your personal visions for older adult ministries, and from them, a shared vision should emerge. "A shared vision is not an idea. . . . It is, rather, a force in people's hearts, a force of impressive power."[2]

When people share a vision, they are connected, bound together for a common purpose. Your council needs to put into words what you see your vision for older adult ministry to be (this is often called a "mission" or "vision" statement). Only when you can state it (and in as few words as possible) will you know whether you are on the right path to achieving your vision.

Step 6: Develop a program of ministry for your congregation.

After you have interviewed the older adults in your congregation (and community where this is practical), have evaluated existing church/synagogue programs and accessibility, and have identified community social service agency programs, you are now ready to develop a ministry with older adults.

Keep in mind the primary task of the local congregation. Identify ways you can reach out in ministry to the older adults in your congregation and community, helping them in their relationship to God, nurturing them in the faith, and equipping and supporting them as they live out their lives as persons of faith in their families, community, and world.

Step 7: Identify resources and key persons.

After you have identified the programs or ministry most needed, you will need to identify the resources and key persons which can help you realize your goals. Some questions to keep in mind are these:

- What resources are needed to get the job done?
- Where can you turn for assistance in getting the necessary resources?
- Who can best help you implement your program?
- Who is most capable of providing leadership?

The council will need to discuss the best possible resources and key persons for the program. Be thorough and resourceful; "leave no stone unturned." As you review your program needs, identify and seek out the best resources and most qualified persons.

Step 8: Where appropriate, involve other faith communities and social service agencies.

You don't have to try to do everything yourself. Sometimes we discover that our resources are not great enough or that we are better able to get the work done by involving other churches/synagogues and/or social service agencies. Identify and invite other congregations and agencies to become involved. Combine forces for getting the program started and to keep it going.

Today just as businesses are learning that total quality management involves cooperation and not just competition, congregations will want to see the larger picture in ministry with older adults. Our concern is for the well-being of older adults and the community as a whole. Competition has no place where meeting the needs of older adults is a primary focus. Simply stated, do not compete for the same audience, but work together wherever possible.

Step 9: Implement your program.

Begin by establishing a timeline for implementing your older adult ministry. Identify the various steps along the way. Make a flowchart to help you identify and understand the process involved in your system of older adult ministries or a specific program. List the resources to be used and the outcome you want to achieve. This is your check list, or memory jog, as you implement your program. It will help you make sure your vision for older adult ministries is being realized.

Step 10: Evaluate.

Periodically evaluate the program and process to make sure you are accomplishing what you set out to achieve. This is a good way to determine the effectiveness of your program. Listen to the voices of the people you are serving. Are they receiving the desired results? Are there gaps in the process? Are persons growing in their faith and spiritual well-being? Are lives being transformed because of your ministry?

In an effort to evaluate your older adult ministries, learn how to listen. Use surveys, one-on-one conversations, focus groups, and other means for getting feedback. The more information you receive, the better your chances will be for developing and implementing a viable and successful program that meets and exceeds the expectations of persons involved in your older adult ministry.

Quality is important to any consumer. Continuous improvement is vital to the success of businesses. Likewise, congregations need to be aware of the importance of quality in meeting the needs of the people. As you receive feedback, continue to improve your program. If you discover, through feedback, that your program is not working, begin the process over again.

Chapter 5

LEADERSHIP IN OLDER ADULT MINISTRIES

A little boy was intently watching television. Suddenly he stopped, turned to his mother, and asked, "Mommy, are we *live* or are we just on tape?"

When it comes to leadership in older adult ministries, this is an appropriate question for the church and synagogue to ask themselves. Are the church and synagogue *live* to the need for recruiting and training adequate and quality leadership for effective ministry with the aging, or are we just on tape? Do we clearly see:

The who of leadership (the types of persons who could be recruited for quality leadership),

The what of leadership (the responsibilities of leaders in older adult ministries), and

The how of leadership (training models) in the development of quality leadership for effective ministry with older adults in congregations? Let us begin this appropriate quest.

The Who of Leadership

A wide range of individuals are potential members for Older Adult Councils, committees, or task forces designed to develop and implement programs of ministry with older adults. These include:

Older persons themselves (those sixty-five years of age and older). Congregations of all faiths are increasing in numbers of older members. In fact, mini-conferences on spiritual well-being previous to the 1995 White House Conference on Aging reported that the population of older adults in religious congregations across the United States continues to increase at a rate faster than the population at large. Many of these persons now in their retirement or new leisure years have rich backgrounds of experience in many areas of service.

Therefore, a special effort should be made by congregations to discover the talents of these individuals and make use of them so they are enabled to give creatively of themselves and their abilities in planning or programming.

Clergy (ministers/pastors, priests, rabbis). More and more clergy are placing a high priority on developing effective programs of ministry with older adults in their congregations. Their leadership and guidance as "spiritual shepherds" is a great and necessary resource for Older Adult Councils, committees, or task forces. If clergy in a congregation are not involved in some fashion, then older adult ministries are not likely to have the moral and financial support they need.

Lay leaders (leaders in church/synagogue councils and boards, men's groups, women's groups, religious education programs, committees and task forces for action, etc.). Such leadership should desire to bring about a better understanding of older adults and the aging process in life which enriches the intergenerational society in which we live. They should be committed to planning and implementing effective and meaningful programs of ministry with older adults. When lay leaders in a congregation who have the power of leadership are not involved in some fashion, then older adult ministries are not likely to have the moral and financial support they need.

Young persons. More and more young persons are realizing they need to be involved with older adults in planning older adult ministries, for they are aging and will become a generation of older adults in the future. Older adults are seeing the need for help from youth so that any older adult ministry can be an intergenerational effort and concern. This was shown in the 1995 White House Conference on Aging when for the first time twenty youth delegates were present to help plan aging priorities and programs which would affect the twenty-first century.

Perhaps this awareness on the part of young persons and older adults is coming about because youth are seeing the aging process to be a normal one and not to be feared and older adults need to face this same vision.

Happily, some teenagers and older adults are discovering how much they have in common and how much they mutually need each other in ministry. For instance,

- The young are striving for a meaning in life; the old are striving for a meaning in life.
- The young are seeking to train themselves for the first stages in life; the old are seeking how they might train themselves for "the third age," the retirement-leisure-creative giving stage of life ("the first age" being childhood and youth and "the second age" being the work years of adulthood).
- The young have a real interest in the sexual experience in life; the old have a renewed and real interest in the sexual experience in life.
- The young have problems with driver's licenses; the old have problems with driver's licenses.
- The young have difficulties with car insurance; the old have difficulties with car insurance.
- The young question the value systems of society; the old question the value systems of society.
- The young have less power, fewer resources, and less influence than the work force; the old have less power, fewer resources, and less influence than the work force.
- The young are seeking mentors; the old are able to advise and

model appropriate values.

- The young are concerned about the future as they grow older;
the old are concerned not only about themselves in the
future, but also about the needs of youth as they grow older
and become the future generation of older adults. . . .

And on and on we could go listing similarities between the
concerns of the young and older adults.

The "Gray Panthers," founded by the late Presbyterian Church
executive, Maggie Kuhn, are a living example of how the young
and old support each other's needs and concerns through action
projects and task forces. Many congregational councils, committees, or task forces made up of young and older members become
vital examples of intergenerational involvement with each other's
needs and concerns.

Professionals (active and "recycled). Those with professional
expertise in any field can be helpful in an effective ministry with
older adults–doctors, lawyers, teachers, dentists, nurses, librarians,
home economics specialists, dietitians, legislators, social workers,
opticians, business managers, ministers, church executives, mission-
aries, chaplains, to name a few. These professionals may be active
or retired and willing to be "recycled." The potential of this service
force for congregational Older Adult Councils, committees, and
task forces is great.

Technicians-laborers (active and "recycled"). Secretaries,
electricians, plumbers, roofers, carpenters, gardeners, bus drivers,
farmers, and other technicians-laborers may be active or retired
and willing to be "recycled" providing agreements may be made
with unions as needed. Again, the potential here is tremendous for
Older Adult Councils, committees, or task forces.

The Ideal Qualities of Vounteers

Persons willing to give of themselves as volunteers in ministry
with older adults need as many of the following qualities as possible:

1. **A genuine love of people.**
    Toleration should spring from compassion, not from indiffer-
    ence; it should be active, not passive.

2. **A mind which is open to learning.**
   Even if it does consider itself well stocked, a mind should be eager to learn.

3. **An intense personal faith.**
   This faith should be evident in one's work and in the people it concerns. Many people fancy they can convince others without holding any sincere convictions themselves. They simply cannot.

4. **A desire to give and to seek cooperation.**
   The "lone ranger" attitude makes good movie material, but not good social volunteer material. It is better to remember that there are always men and women who can help you. Give them a chance to do it.

5. **The spirit and courage which can dare to experiment.**
   By all means look before you leap, but if you are going to leap, don't look too long.

6. **An ability to inspire others with enthusiasm.**
   It is not enough merely to have conviction and enthusiasm oneself; one must communicate it to others. The world loses much by indifference. It is our job to create divine discontent.

7. **An ability to look and to plan ahead, to use initiative in tackling a job.**
   Don't always wait for necessity to mother invention; see what you can do about it yourself, and ahead of time.

8. **A willingness to revise ideas and plans where necessary.**
   An effective leader is able to cut off dead branches and graft on new shoots. We are apt to become so involved, physically and emotionally, in our own ideas, plans, and projects that we forget to be objectively critical of them, or to notice the march of fresh knowledge and ideas. A worker should not be "too busy" to sit back and think sometimes.

9. **The ability to reduce work and situations to simple terms of action, speech, or approach.**
   This is not as easy to do as it sounds, but it is the best method of getting results. There are two ways of going about every-

thing. One is complex; the other is simple. Both volunteers and "clients" are frightened off or unnecessarily hampered by words and jargon and schemes which are too technical, complicated, and high-sounding.

10. Tenacity of purpose.

The reason the bulldog wins is that he "hangs on." That is what a volunteer worker must learn to do also—hang on, in spite of frustration and setbacks, and win through.[1]

The What of Leadership

No matter what their classification or expertise might be, leaders in congregations cannot accomplish tasks *alone*. They find their real strength in responsible *teamwork*, a sense of being *one* in striving toward common goals. Teamwork calls for planning together, working together, being trained toward a ministry together.

In this case, we are talking of planning, working, and being trained for an effective, meaningful ministry with older adults in congregations and communities through such units as Older Adult Councils, committees, or task forces.

Together, a congregational Older Adult Council, committee, or task force made up of clergy and lay leaders with the biblical/theological foundation of the church/synagogue can bring about:

- The reshaping of social attitudes toward age and the aging.
- The redirecting of social trends involving the elderly, the spiritual preparation of all ages for their older years, and the permeation of the whole congregation and community with reverence for the old and the aging process of life.

Together, a congregational Older Adult Council, committee, or task force made up of clergy and lay leaders can help the church/synagogue to:

- Become an advocate for a system of values for individuals and society which upholds the significance of older adults.
- Act in compassion and understanding toward older adults, protecting them when they need protection, enabling them to give creatively of themselves, and helping them to achieve

their rights and the rights of future generations as human beings who are growing older.

The How of Leadership

Once the task of recruitment is finished, and the responsibilities of leadership in teamwork are clear, then a congregation is ready for training leaders to accomplish the task of effective ministry with older persons.

Teamwork training will be needed on many levels, depending upon the training goals and the scope of training needed. Training events are developed in many ways:

1. Individual congregations sponsor special training events.

2. Clusters of congregations sponsor denominational, interdenominational, or interfaith training events and programs.

3. Regional or state conferences/councils of churches or interfaith coalitions on aging sponsor training events.

4. State offices on aging and area agencies on aging within states sponsor training programs for all who plan to work with and for the aging. The programs are not for church/synagogue leadership alone, but are helpful to such leadership.

5. State associations of homes for the aging or state health care associations sponsor special training events or conferences.

6. State or regional gerontological societies sponsor special training events or conferences.

7. Colleges/universities/seminaries conduct training programs in the field of aging which are most helpful.

8. Gerontological centers in connection with colleges/universities/graduate schools conduct training programs or offer classes in the field of aging from a specialized viewpoint.

9. Many religious bodies offer, on a national or regional level, conferences, workshops, or other training events on ministry with older adults.

Congregations should make every effort to provide scholarships and opportunities for clergy and lay leaders who are part of Older Adult Councils, committees, or task forces to take advantage of available training experiences.

Within a congregation of any faith, there is a rich opportunity to provide training through many designs or models. ***Four designs or models*** that have been used successfully include the following:

1. A Homily to "Build a New Concept of Aging and its God-given Potential."

Although the homiletic approach is seldom seen as a means of leadership training, it is a prophetic means of sensitizing and motivating the development of church/synagogue leaders and programs. Through the homiletic means, church/synagogue leaders of all ages can be urged to be good stewards of their *whole* life as long as they have breath. In our older years, we must be enabled to continue giving of ourselves in constructive activities in behalf of others (so far as we are capable) as well as receiving. This is one of our basic spiritual needs.

2. A two-hour introductory workshop offered by a guest leader or a capable congregational leader.

Objectives in such a workshop should be to enable and empower participants to:

- witness for the important challenge of ministry with older adults through the congregation and begin to make this ministry happen;

- verbalize "a new concept of aging" which will assist them in erasing negative stereotypes of aging among all age groups in their congregation, including older adults who have accepted the myths about growing older and need to be freed by the facts;

- introduce in their congregation/community at least one program model by which older adults can begin to achieve their God-given potential for giving themselves in a "new rhythm of life" through church/synagogue and community; and

- become knowledgeable about resource tools that could assist them as leaders to execute step-by-step procedures in beginning or expanding an effective ministry with the aging.

3. A one-day seminar/workshop on "Ministry with the Aging" led by a guest leader or a capable congregational leader.

Expanding upon the objectives in the two-hour introductory workshop, this model has one of the greatest potentials for accomplishing the most in quality leadership training. It could be sponsored for use in one congregation, a cluster of congregations, or an interfaith group.

- **Theme.**
  Potential themes for the training might be "Congregations Facing the Challenge of Ministry with Older Adults" or "Congregations Exploring the Good Age—Understanding and Enabling the Potential of the Older Years."

- **Room arrangement.**
  This seminar workshop will require:
    - A semi-circle of chairs facing an open wall
    - A flip chart (newsprint) and/or a chalkboard, tables at the front of the room, upon which are displayed selected resources in such categories as:
        a. Understanding Aging
        b. Retirement Education and Life Planning
        c. Death and Dying
        d. Creative Education
        e. Congregations and Aging
        f. Community and Aging,
        g. Health, Nursing Homes, and Hospitals
           (See "Suggested Print and Audio-Visual Resources" at the back of this book.)

Remember, having the resources available at the front of the room makes them easily accessible for the leader to refer to them and lift them up during the session. They are also readily available to seminar/workshop participants during break periods.

- **The approach to a seminar/workshop.**
  Always begin sessions on time and dismiss on time. In all sessions, strive for group involvement in the training, helping par-

ticipants in the training to feel they are an integral part of the process.

• **Resources needed.**
Provide a packet of resource materials for each seminar/workshop participant which would include a copy of this book, *Aging: God's Challenge to Church and Synagogue,* along with any other materials that would be needed in the training process or as extra helps. This would include "Facts About Aging: A Quiz" (see Appendix C), "Facts About Aging: Answers" (see Appendix D), and an evaluation form for the event.

The expense of such materials can be covered by a registration fee or by congregational leadership training funds. Charts should be prepared which give demographic information and key points on the theological base for ministry with older adults. Such information can be gleaned from chapters in this book.

• **Checklist for details:**
❑ Has the seminar/workshop been adequately publicized to recruit the greatest number of trainees possible?

❑ Is the room size adequate for the number of participants expected?

❑ Is the lighting in the room adequate?

❑ Is the room temperature conducive to learning?

❑ Are the charts which are needed prepared so that ALL can read them?

❑ Have audio-visual resources to be utilized been ordered along with appropriate study guides?

❑ Is audio-visual equipment available and ready along with a competent operator? (It should be noted that charts and other visuals used are important. Education specialists have demonstrated that seminar/workshop participants learn much more from what they *see and hear together* in a learning experience.)

❑ Are all resource materials available?

❑ Have adequate personnel and an adequate set-up been arranged for registration?

❑ Are refreshments ready for use during registration and break periods?

- **Suggested schedule.**
  The following schedule is typical for seminar/workshops on weekdays. (Sunday schedule times have been placed in parentheses.)

  9:30 A.M. (2:30 P.M)
  Registration, coffee and fellowship

  10:00 A.M. (3:00 P.M)
  Greetings and devotional moments by the host clergy

  10:20 A.M. (3:20 P.M)
  Introduction to the theme and content by the seminar workshop leader:

  Discovering Our Needs—Who Are We? Why Are We Here?

  Purpose:
  This is a time of getting acquainted with persons in the group and their particular concerns and needs as congregational leaders seeking to be more effective in "ministry with older adults."

  Procedures:
  In a *small group* (fifteen persons or less), ask persons to introduce themselves and indicate their priority concern in ministry with older adults as congregational leaders. As the concerns are mentioned, list them on a flip chart sheet to be taped to the wall in the front of the room (with masking tape) for reference throughout the workshop by the leader and participants.

  In a *large group* (more than fifteen persons), ask persons to form themselves into small groups of no more than five in

59

which they introduce themselves to each other and discuss their individual needs/concerns as leaders for developing effective congregational ministry with older adults. After listing their individual needs/concerns, each group chooses one need from the list which would represent the group's first priority need. This group process takes about ten minutes. Then involve the participants in a *sharing time* when each small group shares its first-priority concerns. As they are shared, the leader records them on a flip chart sheet which is taped to the wall at the front of the room (with masking tape). The posted list of priorities should be addressed in the training design that follows.

11:00 A.M. (4:00 P.M.)
Building a New Concept of Aging

Purpose:
The purpose of this section of the workshop is to assist participants "to get the garbage out of their thinking about growing older," freeing them from myths about aging by knowing the facts, and helping them to answer two basic questions imperative for leaders if they are to develop effective ministry with older adults:

- How do I feel about growing older?

- How do I feel about older people? Only when these questions are faced from the "gut level" can persons be freed to enable themselves and others to live out their potential as they grow older. (For resource information on "a new concept of aging," see chapter 1 in this book.)

Procedure:
Use "Facts About Aging: A Quiz" (see Appendix C) in the following manner:

- Introduce this section of the workshop by sharing the purpose of the section as indicated above. Ask the participants to remove from their resource packet "Facts About Aging: A Quiz." Indicate that the quiz is designed to help the participants face with facts their own aging and their feelings about older people.

- Ask the participants in a few moments to answer each question on the quiz to the best of their ability.

- Then read question #1 aloud along with possible answers provided on the quiz. Ask participants to raise their hands when the answer they feel to be correct is read. This will help the leader and the group to see the answers felt to be correct by the participants. Finally, give the correct answer for the question from the accompanying "Facts About Aging: Answers" (see Appendix D). Discuss the correct answers with the group.

- Move to the next question and follow the same procedure. After the answers to the quiz have all been shared, ask members of the group how well they did. Did they learn something new?

12:15 P.M. (5:15 P.M.)
Break—Time for book display browsing.

12:30 P.M. (5:30 P.M.)
Lunch (Dinner)

1:30 P.M. (6:30 P.M.)
How Does a Congregation Begin/Expand a Ministry with Older Adults?

Procedure:
- Introduce the overall contents of this book, *Aging: God's Challenge to Church and Synagogue,* by pointing out how each chapter becomes a step-by-step guide to effective ministry with older adults, beginning with chapter 1, which helps us to "build a new concept of the potential of growing older." This will help the group to review the learnings they have already experienced so that these learnings may become a foundation for further learning.

- Introduce specifically the step-by-step procedures outlined in chapter 4 of this book on "Getting Started in Older Adult Ministries" in a chart presentation.

- Divide participants into small discussion groups of five or six persons, with each group representing one particular congregation, if possible. Discuss the step-by-step procedures for beginning or expanding a ministry with older adults and what this means for your congregation.

2:15 P.M. (7:15 P.M.)
Break-Time for book display browsing

2:30 P.M. (7:30 P.M.)
The Unique Role of Congregations in Ministry with Older Adults

Purpose:
This portion of the workshop lifts up the "unique role" congregations must be responsible to assume and seeks to assist participants:
- To recognize the spiritual needs of older persons included in this "unique role,"
- To understand the theology of aging,.
- To use program directions and models for older adult ministries which emphasize this "unique role."

(In a weekend retreat on Ministry with Older Adults, a session on "Congregations and Communities Working Together in Older Adult Ministries," such as discussed in chapter 9 of this book, can be added because of the availability of more time.)

Procedures:
Introduce "The Unique Role of Congregations in Ministry with Older Adults" by lifting up "spiritual needs of the aging" (see chapter 2), a theology of aging (see chapter 3), and relevant program models in older adult ministries (see chapters 6, 7 and 8). Remember that you have only one hour to achieve this important purpose.

3:30 P.M. (8:30 P.M.)
Stand-up Break followed by Evaluation
It is helpful to prepare special evaluation sheets where each

section of the seminar/workshop may be evaluated on a scale of one to ten (one being "not helpful" and ten being "very helpful").The form also should leave room for comments on each section of the seminar/workshop and general comments at the end.

3:50 P.M. (8:50 P.M.)
Closing Moments of Challenge and Commitment
In a closing circle, the seminar leader challenges the congregational leaders in the seminar/workshop to commit themselves to the development of an effective and meaningful ministry with older adults that enables and empowers older adults through their congregations.

4:00 P.M. (9:00 P.M.)
Adjournment

4. A weekend retreat on "Ministry with Older Adults" led by a guest leader or a capable congregational leader.
Such a retreat could be an extension of the one-day seminar/workshop including sections on the following:

- Congregations and Communities Working Together in Older Adult Ministries.
- Special-interest groups led by competent leaders with expertise in such areas as:
    a. Advocacy and Older Adults
    b. Creative Education for Older Adults
    c. Liberation and Interdependence of Older Adults
    d. Facing Discrimination Among Aging Persons (including discrimination based on sex and race)
    e. Intergenerational Programming (see Chapter 8)
    f. Death, Dying and Grief
    g. When Parents Grow Old
    h. Pre-Retirement Education and Life Planning, and
    i. Support Services for Older Adults (see Chapter 7).
- Next steps in planning and implementation for a ministry with older adults in our congregation and community.

Chapter 6

PROGRAM DIRECTIONS AND MODELS FOR OLDER ADULT MINISTRIES

Grandma Mapes was approaching her one-hundredth birthday, and all her family and friends were making plans for a gala celebration. "How would you like a ride in an airplane?" suggested one publicity-conscious relative. "I could arrange the flight."

The determined older woman, who had crossed the plains in a covered wagon, quickly replied: "I ain't a-goin' to ride in no flyin' machine. I'll just sit here and watch television like the Lord intended I should."

In light of the changing times which have brought vast advances in world technology coupled with our inability to serve human need, even love one another; in light of the way we have too often dehumanized humankind, particularly the old, the minority, the poor; in light of the way we have lost our identity as creatures of God—what is the responsibility and the challenge facing the church and synagogue in ministry with older adults?

The most important objective for congregations is to give meaning and value to human life, based on a scriptural/histori-

cal foundation coming from a series of covenants with God.
How congregations strive for this objective, particularly when we
are seeking to achieve effective ministry with older adults, is best
described by pointing out program directions and models that are
successfully working within:

- An individual church/synagogue,
- A community or area interfaith body,
- A community or area council/conference of churches, or
- A national religious body program with congregational
  involvement.

Approaches to Bring about
Attitudinal Changes about Aging

The following techniques are being used by congregations to
achieve attitudinal changes about older adults and the aging
process among their members and within their community:

1. Providing for intergenerational experiences involving children, youth, adults, and older adults.

2. Accepting responsibility for older adults in the congregation
   and in the community in cooperation with other groups and
   agencies.

3. Making the total congregation sensitive to needs of older
   adults through creative programs of education (self-help
   groups, intergenerational groups, consciousness-raising
   groups, etc.).

4. Designing and committing physical church/synagogue property to be accessible for older adults.

5. Identifying and effectively utilizing human resources of the
   congregation and total community to serve the needs of
   older adults.

6. Pooling and sharing information and skills in a congregation
   with the community at large to serve the needs of older
   adults.

7. Utilizing the skills and experiences of older persons in congregations and community.

A New and Different Kind of "Conference Call"

"No matter how many in-house services we offered, we weren't addressing the needs of the homebound," said the supervisor of Westchester Jewish Community Services, a non-sectarian family counseling agency.

The agency looked for something that would offset the extreme isolation and the loneliness that developed as outside visitors became fewer for the homebound. They were concerned about people in their young and middle years who were suddenly struck by severe disabilities, and older people who were frail and not able to move about.

A weekly conference call for six to eight people of similar interests commenced, and it was very successful. The calls often became the highlight of the week, and deep friendships developed. The homebound learned from one another, supported one another, and have remained friends for years.

An increasing number of social service agencies are sponsoring similar "telephone" meetings up to eight conference calls a week. It is an affordable way to establish a sense of community for their homebound clients and help them to make friends. The homebound are cautious at first, but soon begin to share their problems, interests, and expectations.

For more information about this project, write Westchester Jewish Community Services, 141 North Central Avenue, Hartsdale, NY 10530.

Talent, Education and Expertise (TEE) Inventory

Congregations are developing an inventory of talent, education, and expertise of persons in their membership and community (including older adults) so they can be used in planning and leading programs and projects with older adult persons (see Appendix F).

Creative Religious Education and Continuing Education

1. Face-to-face communication groups on issues of real importance and personal concern to older adults are being developed by
congregations, some on an intergenerational basis. Groups are created and staffed, some by older adults themselves, in which older
persons can deal openly with their concerns and fears. Once
these issues are exposed, older persons are guided to live satisfac-
torily with them. Critical questions and crises such as these are
addressed:

- The need for prayer in our lives.
- The fear of becoming helpless . . . physically and/or mentally.
- The question of death with dignity along with the unnecessary
  prolongation of life.
- The "just to *be* is a blessing, just to *live* is holy."
- How to discover a dynamic understanding of self-worth.
- The recognition of a new cultural vision of older adults.

A background paper on "Spiritual Well-Being, Ethics, Values, and
Roles" for the 1995 White House Conference on Aging challenges
us with these words:

> *The cultural vision of the Third Age embodying*
> *ideals of a deep and wise spirituality must*
> *encourage older persons to be the moral memory*
> *of society, reminding us of our collective tri-*
> *umphs and contributing mightily to more just*
> *and compassionate homes, neighborhoods, com-*
> *munities, nation and world.*

2. Some congregations are developing **support groups** or **self-
help groups** for the encouragement and liberation of older
women who constitute the majority of older members in most
congregations. Many women have lived in the shadows of their
husbands and children, without discovering their own identity and
worth. When their husbands die and their children move away,
many women become lonely, isolated, embittered, and discour-
aged. Through self-help support groups of the church/synagogue,
these women can find new direction and purpose for their lives.

Their needs are urgent. Pastoral calls may give temporary aid, but self-help support groups give them new life.

3. Some congregations are developing **consciousness-raising groups** (and these should be meeting in every congregation) on an intergenerational basis to increase congregation-wide understanding of age and what it means to grow old in a technological society. These congregations believe that the same concern for the religious nurture of children and youth should be directed toward the nurture of congregations about old age.

4. Some congregations as well as state, area, and national religious bodies are developing **death and dying seminars,** realizing with the famed Elizabeth Kubler-Ross that persons of all ages need to deal with death and ministry to the dying in an environment of frankness, realism, and understanding. (See the "Selected Print and Audio Visual Resources" in the back of this book.)

The issue of "death and dying" can be summarized by the story of Mary, who faced courageously the fact that she was dying of cancer. A friend asked her how she could be so brave and courageous. She replied: "I've spent most of my life showing my children how to live. Now I must show them how to die." What better task can the church/synagogue have among its responsibilities than to teach its people how to show others the way to die?

5. Through a project at Christian Theological Seminary, Indianapolis, Indiana, entitled "Continuing Education: Mental Health of Aging Persons," funded by the National Institute on Mental Health, **personal growth or life enrichment groups** of older adults were created for use in congregational and community settings.

These small life enrichment groups of older adults (intergenerational ones are possible, too) are:

- made up of eight to twelve persons,
- designed to create and encourage *life change* in the participants,
- designed to help each person in the group set *life change goals* by using special resource tools,

- designed to let the group provide counsel as needed, support, encouragement, and opportunity for interchange with group participants.
- held one session per week for at least one hour for at least twelve weeks.

They work! One of the authors knows because he has led one group and watched the effects of many others. The group he led held twelve weeks of sessions for one hour per week over a period of seventeen weeks due to severe winter weather in Indianapolis. The group was tested as they began their life enrichment experience and as it ended. Their test scores were compared to a control group of older adults who had not participated in a life enrichment group. After twelve weeks of sessions (even interrupted), test results revealed that:

- comfort in religious beliefs remained at the highest score possible,
- depression was greatly decreased,
- tension and anxiety were greatly reduced,
- fatigue and inertia levels were greatly reduced, and confusion was significantly decreased in the greatest degree of any measurement.

Primary goals in life change set by each of the eight persons participating in the group were rated on a scale of one to ten as to whether they were reached (with one representing no results and ten representing the goal as fully reached). According to the participants themselves, they reached their life change goals on a scale of four to ten.

For more information on *Life Enrichment Groups, including copies of the special resource tools*, write Donald F. Clingan, national interfaith consultant on ministry with the aging, 41 Westwood Terrace, Springfield, IL 62702.

6. Numerous congregations sponsor active **continuing education programs** which have provided zest for living among many older adults. Classes and lectures are conducted to help older persons deal more effectively with daily living. Examples are courses on consumer education, health education, literacy, writing, retirement planning, defensive driving, estate planning, Bible study, ceramics, yoga, community affairs, foreign languages, home improvement, drama, sewing, cooking for one, travel with a purpose, etc. The number of courses offered and subject matter discussed is limited only by the interests of the older persons themselves and the availability of competent instructors. (See Shepherd's Center model of "Adventures in Learning" in this chapter.)

Worship and Religious Nurture

Congregations are creating opportunities in which older adults can take real, significant, and appropriate roles in celebrative worship and religious nurture. Worship services which are designed to include appropriate modes of expression for older adults and other congregational activities are planned during those hours which are most conducive to widespread older adult participation. These events also are created to express the heterogeneous unity of the congregation, placing older adults in touch with other segments such as young adults, youth, and children where the spirit of each generation may contribute to the other.

Some congregations are celebrating a **senior citizen's Sunday or Sabbath** held at any time of the year. The purpose of the day is to introduce a whole congregation to the cause of older adults in an effective, dramatic way—awakening, inspiring, and reinforcing the spirits of older adults as well as the whole parish.

The suggested format for the day includes a worship service in which there is a guest minister/pastor, priest, or rabbi or a dedicated lay person as the speaker. In the church or synagogue school on that special day, emphasis should be made in classes of all age groups on such subjects as "Why Do We Have Grandmas and Grandpas Anyway?" (for children) or "Older Years Can be Exciting Years" (for youth and adults).

The last service of the day is followed by a congregational dinner with older members of the congregation as honored guests. The meal is followed by a brief program, which includes fun-singing, an audio-visual presentation, or a brief address and challenge.

The Ministry of Elders
(the Unique Ministry of Older Adults)

Congregations are taking up the challenge of a scriptural precedent which calls for using the wisdom and experience of older persons in ministry. In the synagogue and early church, important functions were the responsibility of "elders," who were literally older men and often heads of households.

In both Jewish and Christian communities, elders were responsible for administration and discipline and were religious leaders within the community. Regardless of age, a man was recognized as an elder if he had sufficient maturity and faith to assume this role of leadership. With the scriptural precedent set, some congregations have initiated "the Ministry of Elders," emphasizing not a ministry of the office-elder or a ministry of elders who are men only, but emphasizing instead "the unique ministry of older adults."

This ministry involves older men and women in the creative giving of themselves through congregation and community and is built upon a basic philosophy determined by four important convictions:

1. Older Persons are potentially God's splendid ones.
• Each is a unique person.
• Each is called by God to become personally involved in some way, seeking solutions to the problems that confront us all.
• Each is entrusted with a "job" to do, one that has been given to no one else.
• Our churches/synagogues, communities, nation, and world *need* what each older person has to give.

2. Older persons need a new rhythm in life.
Studies have indicated that older persons need and desire a new rhythm in life that includes (1) short-term giving of oneself in service followed by (2) relaxation and renewal (opportunity for recreation, travel, and study).

3. Older persons need new "adventures in learning" for the creation of new skills and the sharpening of older ones.
The first stages of "Adventures in Learning" and training for "The

Ministry of Elders" usually are offered within the congregational or interfaith setting (see chapter 4 in this book and the "Creative Religious Education and Continuing Education" section of this chapter), but more advanced training is offered by clusters of congregations assisted by theological seminaries, universities, and community service groups with special expertise.

In the training program, special emphasis should be placed on the meaning of the Judeo-Christian tradition and faith; a study of the Scriptures; a study of ethics, social science, and wrestling with many issue of faith and society. Advanced training has as its goal the development of mature Jews/Christians who find joy in communicating with God and sharing in service with others, i.e. prayer and study leading to witness and action.

4. Older persons need a "cafeteria of choices" for the giving of themselves as they are able through church/synagogue and community.

A wide range of opportunity through choices is open to older persons in "The Ministry of Elders" (the unique ministry of older adults). The following suggestions have been collected out of the experiences of the authors of this book. It is only the beginning of even more ideas that will be forthcoming out of the creative thought of committed older persons and religious leaders. We might refer to these suggestions as a "cafeteria of choices" for the ministry of elders.

a. Ministry by older persons for their peers through:

- Friendly visiting. Such programs are mushrooming all over the United States.

- Telephone reassurance. Older persons can be a real help as volunteers in many versions of telecare.

- Companion service. More than transportation, this service provides volunteers who escort persons to the doctor's office, grocery store, Social Security office, etc., helping them every step of the way.

- Home maintenance and repair. A program which enlists volunteers with special skills in home maintenance and repair to assist older adults.

- Meals. Helping to provide Meals on Wheels or group meals programs.
- Outreach. It has been discovered that older persons can better find other persons who need services.

b. Ministry by older persons with congregations through:

- A training program for different church/synagogue offices.
- Older persons have so much to give out of their experience in the training of younger persons for church/synagogue offices.
- Tutoring. Older persons have much to share with children and youth in tutoring and are more patient in the process.
- Calling–all types of calling:
  - evangelistic
  - membership renewal
  - nursing home
  - retirement centers
  - hospital.
- Foster grandparents. Older persons like to share with youth and children, even as youth and children like to "adopt" grandparents.
- Heritage center. Designed to give the opportunity for older persons to share with youth crafts and arts of their generation while youth share their hopes and dreams with older persons.
- Intergenerational study-action groups. Designed to bring older persons and youth together in the study of faith and societal issues, resulting in positive witness and action.
- Cheer ministry. Older persons (even in nursing homes, retirement centers, and hospitals or as shut-ins) giving themselves by sending birthday, convalescent, condolence, anniversary, and other types of cards to members of their congregation at the appropriate times.
- Teaching the Word. Sharing the faith in class/group experiences.
- Counseling younger generations. Older persons have much

to share out of their wisdom and experience.

- A ministry of prayer. Older persons can give in this ministry as long as they have being.
- Leading in worship. Older persons have much to give in religious nurture through worship.

c. **Ministry by older persons for community through:**

- Being consultants in community life.
- Leadership in continuing education. Sharing their life training, education, and experience.
- The "watchdog role" in advocacy (see the model in this chapter on "Congregations and Advocacy for the Aging").
- Crime alert. Older persons notice strange happenings in their neighborhood and report them to the police.
- Helping hand. Older person's homes can become havens to those in distress—both children and older adults.
- Twenty-four-hour crisis counseling. Older persons are most capable in this ministry.
- Day care ministry. Older persons are most capable volunteers in day care centers for children and the elderly.

The "Ministry of Elders," the unique ministry of older adults in their creative years, can become a liberating, joyful experience that all might eagerly anticipate.

Pre-Retirement Education

Congregations are involving themselves in pre-retirement education programs for religious workers and laity which emphasize:

- The philosophy of "the third age" for older people, an age of leisure and opportunity for creative giving of self.
- The importance of pre-retirement planning. It has been discovered to a growing extent that planning for retirement is an educational process, an act of mind-stretching.

At least six specific areas of emphasis should be given consideration in pre-retirement education. They can be set up under the following headings:

1. **Fitness (physical, mental, emotional, and spiritual).**
2. **Finances.**
3. **Place of residence.**
4. **Use of time.**
5. **Continuing education.**
6. **Opportunities for creative sharing.**

For resources in pre-retirement education, see the "Suggested Print and Audio-Visual Resources" at the back of this book. You may also find helpful materials through the retirement seminar program of the American Association of Retired Persons, 601 E Street, N.W., Washington, DC 20049 and through your religious body headquarters and pension offices.

Project: HEAD

An example of what congregations can do is a project developed in Philadelphia, Pennsylvania, by Victorina Peralta while she served as administrator of the Department of Community Services on Aging for Catholic Social Services. Later revised by the National Interfaith Coalition on Aging, it is known as *Project: HEAD–Self-help for the Aging within the Church/Synagogue Setting,* which gives older adults opportunities to direct their own community action programs. It stands for Help Elderly Adults Direct.

This program is preventive, supportive, rehabilitative, and innovative. It is based on the premise that spiritual well-being relates to all areas of human activities. It considers better housing, better income, better nutrition, better transportation, better employment opportunities, better social and cultural opportunities, better legislation, better health, etc., by using a dynamic six-point program (social, health and welfare, education, cultural, leisure time-recreation, civic and political action) which the elderly plan, develop, implement, and evaluate themselves. The elderly are not only consumers, but also the deliverers of the programs and services.

For a manual on Project: HEAD, write Donald F. Clingan, national interfaith consultant on ministry with the aging, 41 Westwood Terrace, Springfield, IL 62702-4618.

Interfaith Volunteer Caregivers Program

This program was established with the counsel of the National Interfaith Coalition on Aging and supported by the Robert Wood Johnson Foundation. Twenty-five pilot projects in seventeen states were created between 1984 and 1987.

In 1987 the foundation started the National Federation of Interfaith Volunteer Caregivers, Inc., to assist in the creation of new interfaith coalitions and to provide continuing support and assistance to established ones. Some 375 additional projects were formed and the number continues to grow.

Projects are centered in an interfaith coalition of *congregations* which through congregation coordinators devise methods of ongoing volunteer recruitment from their congregations and community. The role of the recruited volunteers is to serve the disabled, including the frail elderly, in such areas as these:

- Friendly telephoning (two to three calls per week, ten- to fifteen-minute conversations).
- Friendly visiting (minimum of one visit per week, for about one hour).
- Handyperson (small home repairs, assignment usually completed in one to two visits. The person served, called a "Neighbor," pays for needed parts, etc.).
- Respite assistance (sitter companion to care-receiver, while the caregiver is provided respite; two hours, once per week).
- Shopping (for or with the "Neighbor" to medical or social service appointment; one to two days notice).

In this program, the volunteer caregiver chooses the service(s) he or she wishes to provide, how many "Neighbors" he or she wishes to serve, the area within a community or region he or she wishes to serve, and the length of time he or she wishes to serve.

Training for the recruited volunteers is provided through a central administration under a project coordinator. This central body also keeps in close touch with congregation coordinators.

The projects have been extremely successful in attracting and holding volunteers who serve others. The average interfaith volunteer caregivers project has three hundred volunteers serving seven hundred disabled people and frail elderly.

For more information, write the National Federation of Interfaith Volunteer Caregivers, 368 Broadway, Suite 103, P. O. Box 1939, Kingston, NY 12401.

The Shepherd's Center

The Shepherd's Center is a successful interfaith program for inspiring older persons to help each other. This ministry has spread from its beginning in Kansas City to over one hundred locations nationwide today. The name is one that comes from the support and caring expressed in the Twenty-third Psalm.

The Shepherd's Center began in 1972 under the leadership of Elbert C. Cole. Initially started by twenty-five congregations of the Roman Catholic, Jewish, and Protestant faiths, the center is one example of how many religious faiths may work cooperatively to meet the needs of the community by providing comprehensive services.

The Shepherd's Center has organized the needs of older adults into *four areas*:

1. Life maintenance needs.

All persons must have basic human needs met in order to survive. These needs include adequate shelter, nutritious meals, health care, and financial resources.

2. Life enrichment needs.

As people acquire coping and life-enriching skills, they are able to maintain their maximum level of independent living. Some programs provided by the Shepherd's Center include marriage enrichment courses, field trips, and the "Adventures in Learning" program.

The "Adventures in Learning" program, first conducted at Central United Methodist Church, Kansas City, Missouri, has offered courses on thirty-four to forty-five different subjects. The subjects are limited only by the interests and requests of older persons themselves and the availability of competent and willing instructors.

Enrollment in a term has reached up to eight hundred, with an average of about five hundred in attendance. Some students (and remember, these are older persons) have driven a distance of thirty miles to attend the six- to eight-week term of courses meeting one day a week.

Details on the "Adventures in Learning" program include these important points:

- Registration is for participation in a term, not a specific course.
- Participants attend their choice of the seven to eleven courses offered each hour, from 9:00 A.M. to 3:30 P.M., with the afternoon classes and activities from 1:30 to 3:30 being lighter in nature and content.
- Noon lunch (12:00 noon to 1:25 P.M.) divides the day and includes entertainment, announcements, and recruitment in addition to a major forum program with guest speakers.

3. Life reorganization needs.

As people experience significant changes in their lives, opportunities for life reconstruction or reorganization need to be met. Some programs provided by the Shepherd's Center include support groups for widows, caregivers, and stroke victims; and workshops on Alzheimer's disease and divorce recovery.

4. Life celebration needs.

As persons wrestle with the meaning of life and death, life transcendence or life celebration needs must be met. Some programs provided by the Shepherd's Center include providing sacraments for the institutionalized and homebound, Bible study, worship and prayer groups.

The umbrella organization for all of the centers is the not-for-profit Shepherd's Centers of America (SCA). As the coordinating arm, this organization's primary objective is to encourage the establishment of new centers, support existing ones, and contribute to the national aging network. The organization provides training seminars and offers assistance in many other ways.

For more information, write Shepherd's Centers of America, 68700 Troost, Suite 616, Kansas City, MO 64131-4401.

Ministerial Opportunities in Retirement (MOR)

This program, created by Donald F. Clingan as he retired from being a national church executive and a local pastor in the

Christian Church (Disciples of Christ), recognizes retired clergy as having the potential of being a voluminous resource in the ministry of the church/synagogue they have served and loved for many years. The MOR program invites congregations and regional manifestations of a religious body to use the great resources of retired clergy's expertise and services on a short-term basis.

The program works in this fashion:

1. All retired clergy in a particular judicatory or region are invited annually to enroll in the MOR program by sending in a uniform enrollment form along with a short biography and picture. The biography and picture are used in promoting the MOR program through its newsletter, *More about MOR*. The enrollment form lists some twenty ways retired clergy can assist congregations or regions of a religious body and gives opportunity for the enrollee to list other ways they are willing to give of themselves on a short-term basis.

2. When enrollment forms have been received by a central office, they are tabulated to discover who is willing to serve and how they are willing to serve.

3. The tabulation of the enrollment form information is shared in regional body communication channels and newsletters.

4. The *More about MOR* newsletter is distributed to all congregations in a region, urging their use of the expertise available. The services of retired clergy in a wide range of areas are available for travel expenses (mileage and hospitality) plus a mutually-agreed-upon honorarium. If services are desired, a direct contact must be made with the retired clergy requested.

If you would like to have further information, contact Donald F. Clingan, national interfaith consultant on ministry with the aging, 41 Westwood Terrace, Springfield, IL 62702.

Congregations and Advocacy for the Aging

John Gunther, author of *Inside America*, asked Governor Blue of Iowa to name the most powerful group for advocacy in his state. He thought deeply, then replied: "The United Methodists, but they don't know it."

Yet some congregations, clusters of congregations, national religious bodies (such as the National Interfaith Coalition on Aging, now a unit of the National Council on the Aging, Inc.; the Forum on Religion, Spirituality, and Aging of the American Society on Aging; Shepherd's Centers of America; and the National Federation of Interfaith Volunteer Caregivers, Inc. (known as the *National Four*) do know the power they must wield in behalf of older Americans. It was the National Four that lobbied for the inclusion of the issue of spiritual well-being on the agenda of the 1995 White House Conference on Aging and achieved that goal.

There are at least three roles in advocacy that must be accepted by church/synagogue religious bodies at all levels:

1. The watchdog role.

Being observers in hospital emergency rooms, city council meetings, school board meetings, departments of social welfare, prisons, police departments, agencies on aging, legislative chambers, the halls of Congress, the courts on all levels, etc., to be sure that justice is being done not only for older adults, but for *all* persons.

2. The educational role.

Forming study groups which seek knowledge on legislation; welfare rights; those rights belonging to the aging, handicapped, and poor; discrimination toward the aging and minority groups; dehumanizing factors in our society, etc., so that these issues might be faced with full intelligence and action.

3. The advocacy-action role.

On the basis of the "watchdog role" and the "educational role," working for justice and human dignity and human rights. This may take the form of (1) a letter-writing, telegram, or telephone-calling campaign to public officials and other persons of influence who can bring about change, (2) organizing delegations to visit public officials and other persons of influence to achieve action, and (3) preparing signed petitions for change and presenting them to appropriate officials calling for action.

Ministry with the Homebound

When First Christian Church, Springfield, Illinois, realized that they had at least sixty homebound members who needed to feel more a part of the church family, a new "Ministry to Homebound" was initiated, including some services already provided. The new ministry was *five-fold* as follows:

1. *A parish nurse program* was designed to augment the calling done by the church ministers upon church members, to do follow-up calling upon those church members who are dismissed from the hospital, to provide blood-pressure clinics on the first Sunday of the month, and to make the congregation's members aware of health issues. The person holding the position was a retired registered nurse. She required no remuneration except for travel expenses.

2. *Communion was served by the elders* of the church on every Sunday for those church members in the hospital and those homebound members requesting it.

3. *A tape ministry* was available to all shut-ins who requested it. Through a gift, tape players and tapes in the quantity needed were purchased. Tapes of each Sunday morning worship service (including only the anthem, Scripture, and sermon) were made and duplicated in the quantity needed. These tapes were distributed by elders who served these shut-ins communion or by the minister in his calling. As one tape was delivered, the previous one was picked up and returned for further use. Tapes were also available for sale to church members as a whole.

4. *The minister called upon each homebound member* every other week if calling was requested. At first the calls were once a week on Fridays, but as the number of requests for calls rose from twenty to forty, the calls had to be made every other week. This ministry was not only rewarding to the homebound member, but also to the minister. Unless there was a need for a longer visit, the calls were limited to fifteen minutes. Appointments with the homebound were made by telephone so they knew the time and the day the minister would arrive. If for any reason the regular calls could not be made, the minister made every effort to telephone the affected homebound member or write them a note.

5. *A telephone ministry* was established where church volunteers were matched with homebound members who requested the service. Telephone callers agreed to phone the homebound at least once or twice a month. This developed some real friendships; often the callers telephoned many more times than required.

The key to the success of this ministry was that the homebound were notified at the beginning of each year about the different services available to them. *They chose the services they desired, and the church lived up to its responsibility in providing these services in a caring way.*

Other models for ministry with older adults are found in chapter 7 (Caregiving) and chapter 9 (Uniting Generations).

Chapter 7

CAREGIVING:
A ROLE OF
CHURCH AND
SYNAGOGUE

More people are living longer today. Increased longevity and life expectancy are a result of many factors, including better health care and nutrition, advanced medical technology, and job safety. Instead of dying suddenly, older adults may experience increasing dependency. Living longer increases the chance of older adults experiencing debilitating ailments such as arthritis and Alzheimer's disease or being slowed or incapacitated by strokes or heart disease.

Who Are the Caregivers?

Contrary to the myth of family abandonment of older persons, most older people are not lonely and isolated from their families. Often, caregiving responsibilities are assumed by spouse and family members. The majority of primary caregivers of older people are women—wives for men and daughters or daughters-in-law for women. In a study reported by the National Council on the Aging, approximately seventy-five percent of the caregivers were women.[1] While more men are becoming involved in caregiving roles, they generally assume primary care responsibilities when a female relative is unavailable.

While many primary caregivers of older people tend to be spouses, other family members increasingly play a major role. Family assistance initially tends to be financial, such as gifts of cash; and emotional, through visiting, companionship, advice-giving, and phone checkups. As their relative's health declines and needs increase, families provide more concrete daily services, such as cooking, cleaning, shopping, bathing, dressing, feeding, and transportation, often struggling to maintain two households.[2]

Six Trends Affecting Family Caregiving

The role of the family in caregiving is important. However, there are significant changes occurring in traditional patterns of family life that affect this important role. We have identified *six trends affecting family caregiving*.

1. Fewer family members available to share in caregiving.
While the number of families providing care to older relatives is expected to increase substantially in the next few decades, there will be fewer family members available to share in caregiving of aging parents. With declines in birthrate and family size, older adults will have fewer available siblings to provide assistance. As a result, adult children may find the burdens of caring for older parents to be greater.[3]

2. Long-distance caregiving.
Because of changes in lifestyle and mobility, many children live at a great distance from their aging parents. In some cases this is a result of adult children moving to new locations for job and career opportunities. In others, older adults may relocate in later life because of personal desires, health, and economic concerns. Regardless of the reason, providing caregiving by adult children who live many miles and several states away from a frail parent can be a major challenge.

3. Changing family network.

Another trend affecting the role of caregiving on the part of the family is the changing family network. Divorce and remarriage has increased the number of blended families in our society today. "Adult children may thus be caring not only for their biological parents and parents-in-law from their current marriage, but, if previously divorced, may be emotionally tied to their former spouse's parents, especially through the children of the earlier marriage."[4]

4. Competing responsibilities of simultaneous caregiving.

The fastest-growing segment of the older population is age one hundred and over. As a result, many adult children may be faced with competing responsibilities of simultaneously caring for aging grandparents, parents, and children. It is conceivable in the near future that more and more adult children will bear the burden of multigenerational caregiving. "The 'empty nest' is being filled by the frail elderly and by grown children who cannot afford to leave or who return home."[5]

5. The changing role of women.

The changing role of women in our society is another trend affecting caregiving. "Women are assuming new roles and new careers that affect their willingness and ability to meet the needs of aging relatives."[6] In addition to the conflicting demands of work and caregiving, many women are employed because of family financial needs. With the increased number of women in the work force, there is less time for middle-aged daughters and daughters-in-law to care for aging parents.

6. The emphasis upon self-fulfillment.

A final trend affecting the role of family caregiving is the growing emphasis upon self-fulfillment. "Increasing numbers of middle-aged Americans are launching second careers, returning to college, seeking to revive romance and marriage, or traveling abroad."[7] Conflict arises between the needs of aging parents and the options of mid-life and realizing unmet dreams.

The Role of Church and Synagogue in Caregiving

Christians and Jews alike sum up the whole of the law in two great commandments: love of God and love of neighbor. In addition, they both articulate a list of Ten Commandments which includes the commandment to honor your father and your mother. While caring for your aging parents is both legitimate and praiseworthy, we have identified several trends that make this more difficult within our society today. As a result, the need to love our neighbor and our parents takes on an added dimension in our world today.

There are more than five million health-impaired older adults in our society who cannot do such essential daily activities as bathing, feeding, shopping, or dressing. In addition, many of these older persons have chronic disabilities and live alone with no one to depend on for daily assistance. It is estimated that eighty percent of the care now being given to the frail elderly comes from informal sources such as spouses, children, relatives, and friends. However, these informal caregivers usually undergo such stress and personal sacrifice that in isolation this source of support takes a terrible emotional and financial toll on the caregivers.

Caring for an aging parent, relative, or friend can test the most dedicated person. Often there is only one family member available to care for the older person and they may have a family of their own and a job! The local church/synagogue needs to support the efforts of these caregivers and where there is no primary caregiver, they may need to step forward and take on this responsibility.

The National Interfaith Coalition on Aging has identified a model for caregiving which has a least four tiers. While we want to center in on the role of the church and synagogue which is the third tier, let's first look briefly at all four tiers.[8]

First Tier

The first tier is the support of the immediate household of the frail person—spouse, children, siblings, or unrelated persons who live in the same household. This is where the bulk of the care is done now and will continue to be done, and this usually includes some physical caregiving as well as some responsibility for emotional well-being.

Second Tier

The second tier is the extended family and friends network. If the household caregiver is a spouse or sibling, this is the point at which the adult children, nieces, nephews, cousins, aunts, and uncles may be called upon for both physical and emotional caregiving. In the absence of family or along with family, neighbors and friends often provide this assistance on an informal basis as well.

Third Tier

The third tier is formal cooperation between the church/synagogue and local community programs. This is usually used in conjunction with the household and family efforts. However, in the absence of family or any other informal network, this may become the first tier.

Fourth Tier

The fourth tier must continue to be some form of governmental programs. Attempts by the government to shift more of this financial burden on the "private sector" have proven to be infeasible, to say nothing of unjust. While these efforts may have resulted in a raised consciousness about the issue, they have forced more caregiving on family, religious, and neighborhood networks.

The role of the church and synagogue in caregiving is vital. When families are willing to care for the elderly, we need to be supportive. When we broaden our definition of caring, we relieve families of much of the trauma that surrounds the need to ask for other kinds of help.

Most families attempt to maintain their older members at home as long as possible, often at considerable personal sacrifice. "The primary reason for families' desire for assistance is that long-term caregiving is physically, financially, and emotionally burdensome."[9] Churches and synagogues have a God-given responsibility to reach out in helpful ways.

How the Church and Synagogue Can Be Involved in Caregiving

Most families try to care for older relatives on their own. When they reach some crisis or breaking point, they often resort to institutionalization. Often this entry point into a nursing home or retirement community is premature. Had additional resources been known and made available, older adults might have been able to maintain some degree of independence apart from institutionalization.

For a variety of reasons, family members are not always aware of the services available in the community. An important role for any church or synagogue is to appoint a volunteer or staff person to have oversight of the caregiving ministry. This person, who would serve as a coordinator and work with a committee, would have knowledge about available services and resources within the church/synagogue and community.

Involving older adults in the caregiving ministry is a useful way for them to exercise their covenant in service for God. Finding useful activities appropriate to their talents is a key factor in making any caregiving ministry successful. Older adults often have the time, energy, and experience to make an important impact on the needs of others.

Areas of involvement for the caregiving ministry of a church or synagogue may include the following levels of services:

Telephone reassurance

Volunteers from the church or synagogue as well as homebound persons themselves can provide an important contact with others through use of the telephone. A telephone reassurance ministry involves calling and checking on persons on a regular or daily basis. If an emergency arises, the volunteer caller is trained to know what appropriate steps should be taken. Perhaps in the future, with new innovations in telecommunications and computers, telephone reassurance will be replaced through computer networking.

Tape ministry

Volunteers record on audio or video tape worship services and other special events of interest to older adults. These tapes are then taken to the homes of older adults; here they have an opportunity to see and/or listen to the recorded events. Older adults have an opportunity to keep in touch with the worship services of their church or synagogue and to experience other activities without actually being there. Volunteers should check with the persons receiving the tapes to make certain they are knowledgeable about the use of the video or audio cassette equipment.

Special worship and activity services

Many frail and homebound persons are not able to attend regular worship services. Planning and conducting worship services and other religious activities at times other than those normally held provide frail and homebound older adults with the opportunity to worship in their church or synagogue. A monthly Saturday or Sunday afternoon worship service in the church or synagogue with special accommodations for homebound needs may be appropriate.

The worship service might be shorter in length and could include the use of large-print bulletins, as well as traditional hymns, prayers, and liturgy. Special assistance should be provided for the use of rituals such as in receiving communion in the Christian faith as well as maintaining life-cycle traditions and events within Jewish tradition. Volunteers and family members could help transport older adults to the church or synagogue for these special events. Remember to include the choir or cantor and other regular features of the worship service.

Visitation

Older adults who are not able to get out need the social contact of others. Volunteers visiting in the home, hospital, or nursing home is an important way for the church or synagogue to maintain contact with older members. Encourage visitors to listen to the needs, concerns, and stories of the persons they are visiting. A good listener goes a long way in providing important caregiving services to a person who is lonely, sick, or homebound.

Respite care services

Volunteers agree to spend time with a homebound person. This may be from one to several hours, giving the primary caregiver a few hours of respite to do things outside the home. Studies have shown that primary caregivers may experience a high degree of stress and related depression. A common complaint among family caregivers is that the elderly person's needs take up too much of the caregiver's time. Volunteers provide a valuable service for primary caregivers by giving them a time of respite from their ongoing and seemingly endless duties in caregiving.

Companion services

This level of caregiving service involves more than simply visitation. Social contact, accompaniment on walks or errands, and helping with writing letters are some important aspects of this service. Providing transportation and escorting persons to the doctor's office, to the grocery store, and to worship and church/synagogue activities are important functions for volunteers who provide companion services.

Home chore services

Caregiving volunteers provide housekeeping tasks such as laundry, washing floors and windows, vacuuming, sewing and mending, and changing light bulbs. Chore services may also include preparing meals, mowing the lawn, raking leaves, or shoveling snow. Grocery shopping and running other errands is also an important role for home chore service volunteers.

Minor maintenance and repair services

A variety of volunteers with specific skills are essential for minor maintenance and home repair services. This service may include fixing broken steps, painting interior or exterior walls, minor plumbing needs, and faulty electrical fixtures or appliances. It is important to add that in most cases only persons who are trained and skilled in a specific job function, and who are licensed and have liability insurance, should be volunteers for this service. Well-meaning but unskilled volunteers may create potential hazards or major problems.

Parish nurse services

Many churches and synagogues have started parish nurse programs as a way of enhancing their caregiving services. Parish nursing promotes the dignity and wholeness of individuals by assisting persons in understanding the links between faith and health in healing and wellness.

Parish nurses may serve as personal health counselors to members of a congregation, assess health problems, provide emergency care, make referrals, and serve as a liaison with community health-care professionals. The parish nurse works in cooperation with pastors and other church or synagogue staff as a member of the ministerial team to facilitate the church's ministry of health. Parish nurses often are organizers of support groups to help persons cope with special needs, or serve as volunteer trainers to teach persons how to care for sick members of the congregation, to lead discussion and study groups on health concerns.

The parish nurse program utilizes the skills of licensed registered nurses (RN). Many nurses in the program will have completed at least one unit of Clinical Pastoral Education (CPE). Advanced studies and/or a graduate degree plus previous employment in nursing are often required for certification as a parish nurse by many denominations.

Nurses in the parish nurse program may be volunteers or paid staff. They normally supervise the care provided by a home health aide and maintain contact with the physician as the older person's condition changes. In many parish nurse programs, nurses evaluate and review the older person's use of medications, take and record regular blood pressure and blood sugar checks, and administer medication. In addition, they teach other caregivers to do dressing changes and other skilled tasks.

However, in some parish nurse programs, nurses do not provide hands-on nursing, such as giving injections or drawing blood, but function as health educators, health counselors, resource and referral persons and facilitators of support groups.

Accessible church and synagogue buildings

Along with your trustees or other church or synagogue officials, review your building for accessibility needs. Do you have a ramp or elevator if steps prevent accessibility into and within your building? Are the restrooms accessible? Is the lighting bright enough and the acoustics clear enough for all to see and hear? Do you have large-print Bibles, worship aids, and study materials? Are the times of your worship, study, activities, and meetings appropriate to the needs of your older adults? Is your parking lot and entrance areas safe and well-lighted?

Making your building as accessible as possible provides older adults with the opportunity to continue to worship and enjoy social contacts with others.

Church or synagogue resource library service

Providing information about aging and older adult concerns is an essential service. Having a resource library that contains books, videos, audio tapes, and pamphlets about caregiving needs can be a valuable service for caregivers and older adults. Updated information about Social Security, Medicare, and Medicaid should be on file. In addition, information about nursing homes, retirement communities, congregate housing, and other alternative living arrangements should be available.

Caregiver support group services

Churches and synagogues can establish caregiver support groups. Support groups provide individual peer counseling. Primary caregivers find that many of their feelings of guilt, anger, loneliness, and fear are shared by others. Valuable information about referral services and community resources can be learned. Workshops and seminars for caregivers can be provided by medical professionals, hospital staff, long-term care facility staff, and home care agencies. Meeting on a regular basis, primary caregivers receive emotional support and guidance as they adapt to changes and meet the growing demands of caring for loved ones.

Senior banquet services

Once or twice a year a banquet honoring the older members of your church or synagogue could be held. Special transportation should be arranged so that all older adults are able to attend. Entertainment and meal could be enjoyed by older adults who are no longer able to leave their homes. Showing slides or videos of church or synagogue activities and including pictures of young and older members can help brighten the life of any older adult. Being creative is an important ingredient for any successful senior banquet. A planning committee should include older adults themselves.

Adult day care services

Establishing an adult day care service is another opportunity for caregiving ministry by a local church or synagogue. Volunteers, often older adults themselves, can provide this service on a half-day basis, several times a week. This program gives older adults the opportunity to socialize with others in an engaging environment. Games, crafts, music, exercise, learning opportunities, friendly listeners, and special programs may all comprise the daily agenda.

Many churches and synagogues have the good intention of starting an adult day care program. It sounds like an easy assignment. You develop a program offering families a daily respite from caregiving duties. However, each state has a complex set of laws regulating the licensing of day care facilities. Before persons begin, it is important to become familiar with the licensing procedures in your state.

If no medication or physical therapy is administered and no meals provided, an adult day care service program may not require licensing. It is important, however, that participants be able to get around fairly well on their own. A snack may be provided by the church or synagogue or brought from home. A volunteer, or part-time staff member, can usually oversee the program.

Another option is to develop a satellite adult day care center. This program offers frail older adults the opportunity to participate in stimulating activities as well as receive professional supervision and care. Begin by contacting a hospital, nursing home, or other medical organization to help you establish a satellite program. You will need to contract with the medical center for some or all of the following services: occupational and physical therapists, nursing assistance, special diets, and meal preparation.

With paid staff, this program can operate on full-day basis, one or more days a week. Although this procedure simplifies licensing requirements, it also requires a much greater financial commitment on the part of the church or synagogue.

Chapter 8

UNITING
GENERATIONS

Persons of all ages living, growing, working, and playing together is a hopeful concept. Children receiving love and learning faith and values from older adults, and older adults experiencing a sense of being needed and enjoying the continuity of life are important aspects for any society. However, uniting generations is not an easy task.

The Extended Family

Some persons in our society believe that if we simply go back to when the extended family was the norm, then everything will be okay. Calling for an increased role in the extended family is not enough. We cannot go back to a time "when"—when such a time didn't exist.

The extended family, while existing for many, was not a reality enjoyed by most families. Children, parents, and grandparents have not always had the benefit of living together, of sharing values, knowledge, and supporting one another in our society. The idea of the extended family as the norm in our society is a concept that has been romanticized in the hearts and minds of many Americans.

Unfortunately, many well-intentioned people and organizations wrongly believe that at one time the extended family was the norm in our society. The commonly held belief was that grandparents, parents, and children lived together and formed networks of economic, educational, and cultural interdependence. Grandparents shared their values and experiences with their children, provided care to their grandchildren, and served as a knowledge base for family, religious, and cultural traditions. Parents provided economic support to both their children and their parents. Children shared their energy and enthusiasm with their older relatives and learned to be productive members of society as they participated in family life.[1]

While this concept about our past may hold fond memories for some, it wasn't the prevailing pattern for many people in our society. African-Americans, often at a young age, were forcibly taken from their homeland, put in shackles, brought to America, and sold into the barbarous slave-trading market. They left behind their family, community, and country. Once captured and sold into slavery, they were stripped of their freedom. Even their right to marry and have a family was often forbidden. If they did manage to form conjugal relationships, children conceived were often taken from their parents and sold to other slave buyers.

Willing immigrants coming to America often left behind families, too. While their journey from Europe to America was generally voluntary, families remained behind in the "old" country. Often immigrants settled in communities with people from their home country. Sometimes these included the extended family with parents and grandparents. But this wasn't true for everyone.

Horace Greeley said, "Go west, young man," and many young men and women headed westward. They went seeking adventure and the fulfillment of their hopes and dreams. They left their homes, their communities, and in many cases their families and moved to the western sections of the United States. This migration and westward expansion not only disrupted the lives of extended families in the East and Midwest, but also disrupted the lives and families of most Native Americans.

Likewise, many Hispanics and Asian-Americans came to America seeking increased opportunities. Many were young people seeking a better way of life. They, too, often left families behind when coming to America. Establishing a bright future was not always easy within a strange and sometimes forbidding land. Families formed, but they did not always include parents and grandparents. Sometimes families were made up of aunts, uncles, and cousins. Sometimes they were mere acquaintances who became their extended family.

Some people did live in extended families, but many did not. While cultural diversity often brought families together for common bonding, many families were shaped and reshaped by the prevailing changing culture and the reality of a shortened life span. In addition to high incidence of infant mortality, the death of women during childbirth brought about many blended families. Due to poor working conditions and lack of medical care, many persons simply did not reach old age. While many parents did care for both their children and their aging parents, most did not.

All of this is to say that perhaps there never has been a time in America when the extended family was the norm. This is especially true in our own day. As a result of education, job opportunities, and marriage, many young people are moving to other parts of the country. Many families and communities are losing their children because the opportunities for growth are not readily available. Even in times of our depressed economy when many young people are unable to establish financial independence (resulting in some returning or remaining longer in the home), there is not enough evidence to indicate a slowdown in society's mobility.

Older adults, too, are experiencing the freedom of mobility. Many older adults are moving to enjoy a more temperate climate for health reasons or to pursue greater educational or leisure opportunities. Some are starting new careers or are taking advantage of a new housing arrangement or are moving closer to their children or friends. As our society becomes more and more mobile, opportunities for interaction among the various generations continues to decrease.

An Age-Segregated Society

Another problem in uniting the generations is the fact that we live in an age-segregated society. From an early age, we learn to spend much of our time with persons whose situations are very much like our own.

Children spend their days in school with other children. They are age-segregated in their classes beginning with preschool, grade school, middle school, high school, and often even college. Children learn how to play with other children and participate in age-segregated and sometimes gender-segregated civic and athletic activities.

Young families often move into neighborhoods where other parents with young children live. They share baby-sitters, take turns carpooling, and participate with other parents in school and athletic events. They will even commiserate together about their struggles in marriage, jobs, and raising families.

Adults work in workplaces with other adults. They participate in worship and study classes with adults. They serve on religious, civic, and school committees with other adults. People they often meet while shopping, at the doctor's office, or the automobile repair shop are adults.

Many older adults live alone. Sometimes they reside in "seniors-only" communities where children are welcome only for a short time. At church or synagogue they often participate in study groups with adults close to their own age. They may even participate in special activities at social centers which are held for older persons.

As a result of age-segregation, the old fear the young, the young don't understand the old, and society suffers from a growing tension between the generations.

The Church and Synagogue

One institution in our society where intergenerational activity can easily be encouraged is the local church or synagogue. Yet, many churches and synagogues don't even think about the importance of intergenerational relationships. When you walk through the doors of the church or synagogue, you go to your age-segregated groupings. "We have church school classes for the young, some-times further divided by grade level; youth programs; young adult groups; and 50+ organizations. With the exception of the Children's Moment, the service of worship is generally geared to adults only."[2]

Intergenerational thinking and programs do not depend only on the extended family. An African proverb states that "the real bond is not between children and their parents; it's between chil-dren and their grandparents." *(Source unknown)* Grandparents help children grow. That's part of their job in this world. But, in our day, when families live apart and many children rarely see or know their grandparents, faith communities must help older adults catch a vision that all children are their grandchildren!

Since children are often cut off from their grandparents by geography, the result of our highly mobile society, our best hope for the future is to bring the generations in our churches and syna-gogues together. Older adults with a myriad of skills, knowledge, and experiences can be teachers and mentors to young people. They provide a sense of stability and continuity in an uncertain and changing world. Older adults, as the purveyors of faith, can help instill religious values in the lives of young people.

The young, too, have much to offer older adults. Children and youth have new ideas and skills which aren't encumbered by the burdens of traditional thinking. Young persons provide older adults with a sense of presence and connectedness. Young per-sons also provide older adults with the opportunity for what Erik Erickson called "generativity," the desire to help guide the next gen-eration.

Bringing the generations together is a delicate process. Churches and synagogues must ensure that intergenerational con-tact is developed under the best of conditions, without competi-tion and with a sense of shared purpose. Rather than each genera-tion seeing itself as a separate community, intergenerational con-tact allows persons of every age to be an integral part of one larger community. In a time of diminishing resources, uniting genera-tions is particularly important.

What would happen if the generations began seeing them-selves as one big family? If cultural and racial diversity did not get in the way of generations caring for and about one another? What would happen if older adults, using their years of experience, began tutoring schoolchildren, caring for persons with AIDS/HIV, or teaching financial management to young families? What if older adults began serving as foster grandparents for children who had no grandparents or whose grandparents lived too far away? What do you suppose would happen if children visited lonely nursing home residents? What would happen if youth provided a service of raking leaves, mowing grass, shoveling snow, or running errands for older neighbors?

What would our communities be like if adults helped older adults with minor home repair so that older persons could maintain some degree of independence? If older adults and young people together addressed a special need in their community? Instead of segregating the generations, so that only the myths and stereotypes are known, what would happen to our society if the generations came together for the purpose of learning, growing, sharing, and loving?

Getting Started

There are at least four steps in developing successful intergenerational programs. The steps, outlined below, serve as a guide in developing intergenerational programs for your church or synagogue.

1. Define the program

Identify the specific needs of children, youth, families, and older adults in your church/synagogue and/or community. Identify available resources and establish priorities. After you determine the needs and identify available resources, consider what your group would like to accomplish and the goals you want to reach.

2. Develop the program

Plan the appropriate program to meet the specific needs for reaching your goals. Determine what costs are involved and identify ways you can financially resource your program. List the tasks to be performed and secure the necessary resources. At this stage it is helpful to prepare a program outline, including budget costs and timeline for completion.

3. Implement the program

Enlist the support of your faith community. Recruit and train volunteers. Select appropriate personnel to implement your program. Coordinate the tasks to be done in reaching your goals. Promote and publicize your program. Establish evaluation procedures.

4. Evaluate the program

Collect, organize, and interpret feedback information. Evaluate the effectiveness of the program. Continue the program, if it is warranted, or start a new program by beginning the planning process again.

Intergenerational Resources

In order to help unite generations, there are many helpful resources available. The American Association of Retired Persons (AARP) has put together two valuable resource manuals that provide information on ways to start intergenerational programs, as well as a list of models now being used. The resources are free and can be obtained by contacting this organization at American Association of Retired Persons, 601 E Street, N.W., Washington, DC 20049.

Some suggested resources are: (1) *Connecting the Generations: A Guide to Intergenerational Resources*. This is an overview of several intergenerational programs and selected listing of books, manual, and media resources. (2) *Intergenerational Projects: Idea Book*. Successful intergenerational projects ranging from basic tutoring projects to a sophisticated corporate-based day care center are highlighted in this resource.

Program Models

In addition to the models identified by AARP in its resource manuals listed above, the following additional program models are examples of intergenerational programs.

AgeLink

Older volunteers participate in school-age child care, sharing their crafts, helping with homework, supervising games, and listening. *Contact*: Center for Improving Mountain Living, Western Carolina University, Cullowhee, NC 28723.

Cassette Pals

Cassette tapes are exchanged between children and adolescents and homebound elderly. *Contact*: Central Branch RSVP, 406-B West Ridge Pike, Conshohocken, PA 19428.

Family Friend Program

Older volunteers are trained to assist families with severely ill and disabled children by providing activities for the children and support for the parents. *Contact*: National Council on the Aging, 600 Maryland Avenue, S.W., West Wing 100, Washington, DC 20024.

Folk Art Fair

Older craftspeople demonstrate skills, like washing on a washboard, yodeling, and traditional crafts in a school fair. Children participate in hands-on demonstrations with older adults. *Contact*: RSVP of Dane County, 540 West Olin Ave., Madison, WI 53715.

Friendship Across the Ages

Campfire youth and older volunteers pair up and do activities together for at least six months. Program guide available with information on starting a program and suggested activities. *Contact*: Campfire, Inc., 4601 Madison Avenue, Kansas City, MO 64112.

Gramma's Day Care Center

Program is specially designed to care for children with a high risk of Sudden Infant Death Syndrome (SIDS). *Contact*: Senior Citizens Service, 1750 Madison Avenue, Suite 350, Memphis, TN 38104.

Linking Generations

A program exploring ways older adults can be involved with young children in child care programs. *Contact*: Linking Generations, 1075 South Euclid Avenue, Sarasota, FL 34237.

Link the Generations with Love,
an Alternative Vacation-time Program

A program designed to forge a link between potential caregivers (children, youth, and adults) and the recipient of caregiving.

Ready-made teaching plans are available to those who will provide training. *Contact*: Links, Wingborne Diaconal Productions, P.O. Box 15130, York, PA 17405.

Magic Me

In cities across the United States and Europe, preteens and teenagers learn skills to communicate more effectively with elderly participants in nursing homes through seminars, role-play, and interaction. Children provide services and companionship while boosting their own self-esteem and confidence and learning how to develop new relationships. *Contact*: Magic Me, 611 Park Avenue, Suite 6, Baltimore, MD 21201.

Project J.O.Y.: Joining Older and Younger

Elementary school project involving children visiting a nursing home and nursing home residents visiting schools. Intergenerational activities include creative arts, oral history, gardening, and "hands-on" activities. Also intergenerational summer camp, in-depth aging awareness curriculum, teacher training, pen pals program, and parent awareness. *Contact*: BANANAS, Inc., 6421 Telegraph Avenue, Oakland, CA 94609.

READAmerica Summer

A national campaign to promote "Read, America!" sponsored by the National PTA, the AARP, ABC/Project Literacy U.S., the American Library Association, and the National Association of Elementary School Principals. *Contact*: READAmerica, 103 North Duke Street, P.O. Box 1641, Shepherdstown, WV 25433.

Teaching-Learning Communities

This model program, in which elders show and demonstrate crafts in elementary schools, has been replicated across the country. Children and older adults set their own goals. *Contact*: Teaching-Learning Communities, 1212 Roosevelt, Ann Arbor, MI 48104.

Y.E.S.: Youth Exchanging with Seniors

This is an interdenominational community-based project which links youth such as Future Homemakers of America and 4-H Club members with community leaders to provide assisted-living services for elderly. The purpose of this program is to promote positive intergenerational relationships between youth and seniors by providing assisted-living services that enhance independent lifestyles of the elderly in rural communities. *Contact:* Y.E.S., Regenerating Rural America, College of Home Economics, Texas Tech University, P.O. Box 41162, Lubbock, TX 79409.

Chapter 9

CONGREGATIONS AND COMMUNITIES WORKING TOGETHER IN OLDER ADULT MINISTRIES

Congregations of all faiths and the whole realm of community services should be as two hands folded together into one purpose–the effective ministry with older adults. Congregations, although they represent the large majority of older adults in faith and practice, should not try to be islands unto themselves in community life. Nor should community service organizations designed to undergird the aging seek to do their task without recognizing the assistance and influence congregations could provide.

With such convictions in mind, the National Interfaith Coalition on Aging, when it was first formed in 1972, committed itself to this objective:

> *To stimulate cooperative and coordinated action between the nation's religious sector and national secular, private and public organizations and agencies whose programs and services relate to the welfare and dignity of aging people.*

Therefore, how can congregations and communities work together in a sense of *teamwork* so that an effective ministry might be generated with older adults?

The National Voluntary Organizations for Independent Living for the Aging (NVOILA), first founded as the Steering Committee of National Voluntary Organizations in connection with the 1971 White House Conference on Aging, became a program unit of the National Council on the Aging, representing these groups:

- organizations designed for retirees,
- organizations representing geriatric interests,
- professional groups,
- youth groups,
- health organizations,
- women's groups,
- minority groups,
- welfare groups,
- labor unions,
- civic clubs, and
- church and synagogue groups.

NVOILA still exists today, determined to establish teamwork in behalf of older adults, helping them to be independent as long as it is best for them as persons. Three categories of basic services were and still are seen as necessary for the independence of older adults in every community. **Only congregations and community organizations working together** can raise the potential of providing adequately and meaningfully these basic services:

Programs of information and referral

Through public media, newsletters, information centers, volunteer programs, and other means, congregations and community organizations can provide older persons with information to help them remain in their own homes including:

1. **Social Security.**
2. **SSI (Supplementary Security Income).**

3. Social service program.
4. Protective services.
5. Consumer services.
6. Counseling services.
7. Health programs.
8. Food stamp eligibility.
9. Housing relocation.
10. Employment assistance.
11. Volunteer programs.

Programs for direct service

These programs can include service to older persons in their own homes or with older adults in a group setting such as in a senior center. Bear in mind the multiplier effect on the well-being of those served when a cluster of services is provided through congregations and community organizations working together:

1. *Consumer issues*
   - Consumer education
   - Cooperative buying

2. *Creative/leisure activities*
   - Adult education
   - Arts and crafts
   - In-home library services
   - Recreation activities
   - Talking books/reading services for the blind

3. *Health*
   - Health education/counseling
   - Home health services
   - In-home physical therapy
   - Mail-order drug services
   - Multiphasic health screening

4. *Housing*
   - Home repair services
   - Housing counseling

5. *Legal services*
   - Conservatorship/guardianship programs

- Financial counseling
- Legal aid
- Tax counseling

6. *Nutrition*
- Congregate meal
- Food stamps
- Home-delivered meals
- Nutrition education

7. *Social support services*
- Adult day care centers
- Chore services
- Counseling services
- Equipment loan
- Escort services
- Foster home care
- Friendly visitors
- Homemaker-home health aide services
- Personal grooming
- Shopping services
- Telephone reassurance
- Transportation services/reduced bus fares
- Driver refresher courses

Programs of advocacy

The first program for advocacy is accomplished by congregations of all faiths working together within a community. Some national religious bodies produce a wealth of information and resources on ministry with older adults. You may want to contact your own religious body or others for guidance.

National religious bodies and their local congregations working together with national public and private organizations and agencies along with their local affiliates can serve as real advocates to help older persons remain in their own homes. For instance, members of congregations and community organizations can work for the development of housing authorities. They can influence local school boards to provide facilities and vehicles for nutrition and transportation programs.

In many cases, the advocacy role can mesh with other special concerns of an organization. For example, an organization concerned with the physically handicapped could work locally and nationally to focus on the elderly's rehabilitation needs. A health organization could work locally and nationally to center on the health needs of older adults, etc. All national organizations–religious, public or private–should undergird and obtain support for particular issues that confront older adults who are members of minority groups or who have special needs.

It is the duty of any congregation or interfaith group to examine the services for older adults that now exist in its community. This could provide an opportunity to work together in developing services which do not exist. Through joint efforts, the skills and energies of older persons themselves may be enlisted along with providing opportunities for older and younger persons to work together, thus bridging the generations.

Another picture of the "Range of Community Services and Opportunities for Older Adults" which should be provided through the joint forces of congregations, public and private organizations, and agencies is seen through Appendix H in this book. You will note that the pictured services move the full range from "independent living" in one's own home to "dependent living" in a nursing home. Included in this scope and not mentioned within the three basic categories of service recommended by NVOILA are retirement housing and nursing home services of all types.

A third picture of the great potential in total community service teamwork is seen in Appendix J in this book. This is a categorized listing and a specific listing of all the possible organizations within a community that can have a role in an effective team ministry with older persons.

Appendix K provides a "Select List of National and International Organizations" in the field of aging with which you should be familiar.

Appendix L gives the addresses for the offices of the Administration on Aging. These offices plus state offices and area agencies on aging within each state can provide voluminous helps to congregations and community.

When women and men of faith enlist the full range of forces

available to us, nothing can keep the congregations and communities of our nation from achieving their highest dreams for those who deserve our concern and ministry—older adults.

Chapter 10

CHALLENGES
OF THE
FUTURE

Identifying trends is complex work. Living in a fast-paced, evolving, and changing society may make such speculation seem pointless. Yet, from what we know about demographic trends, advanced knowledge in the field of gerontology, and the adopted resolutions of the 1995 White House Conference on Aging, there are some predictions we can make with a degree of certainty.

1. The older population will continue to grow.

In 1994, the older adult population numbered over 33.2 million people. Projections estimate that by 2030, the sixty-five-plus population in the United States will double to more than seventy million. The older population will jump from 12.7 percent of the total population to over twenty percent, perhaps as high as twenty-two percent. With the "boomer" generation being identified as persons born from 1946–1964, the first boomers will reach age sixty-five in 2011. For the next twenty-two years, the ranks of older adults will swell. This increase will have a profound effect upon our society.

At the same time, there is a decrease in the percentage of children and youth in our society. Boomers have not been replacing themselves. Although there are twice as many women of childbearing age today as there were in the previous generation, they are having fewer children. "An estimated 20 percent of baby boomers will have no children at all; another 25 percent will have only one."[1]

Projections indicate that by 2030, older adults will outnumber children and youth in our society. Children and teenagers will make up nineteen percent of the total population while twenty to twenty-two percent will be older adults.[2]

2. *The formation of an elderculture will emerge.*

With a decrease in the number of births and an increase in life expectancy, aging "boomers" will help create an *elderculture* in our society. Aging "boomers" will redefine "older adulthood."

Even in terms of chronological age, the boomer generation will redefine aging. Persons age sixty-five to seventy-five or eighty years of age will not be considered older adults but in "late adulthood." Late adulthood will be a continuation of middle age. Being an older adult will not begin until eighty to eighty-five years of age. Probably when boomers reach eighty-five, they will redefine this age as well.

While they cannot escape aging, boomers "will produce *an elderculture reflecting some of the spirit of the 1960's youth culture*."[3] The cultural and spiritual focal point for American society as a whole has long been identified with whatever age bracket boomers have occupied. "The boomers redefine whatever stage of life they inhabit. They have, in fact, already begun to rebuild the later years of life in their own, more youthful image."[4]

While boomers have long had a fixation on self (over community), they are gaining a new sense of responsibility and self-denial. This has led them to see themselves as an embodiment of moral wisdom. As a result, aging boomers will be creative, busy, active, and involved in living during the later years.

3. *People will be retiring later, and many times.*

While there has been a high number of forced retirements in recent years, early retirement will be a thing of the past. Instead, people will retire later, or will retire many times. Even persons who are forced into early retirement will seek new opportunities for employment.

Why? With the decrease in births, making for a smaller work force among younger adults and with declining Social Security and pension benefits, many healthy, active older adults will find it necessary to keep on working. Likewise, society will welcome and encourage the productivity of older adults. The phenomenon of fewer young people entering the work force will compel an increasing number of employers to call older workers back to the job.

In addition, an increase in age-discrimination lawsuits will prompt more businesses to reevaluate their employment practices. This will impact hiring practices through retirement needs and will force business and industry, as well as churches and synagogues, to confront ageism and ageist practices.

Older adults will move from retirement to "rehirement." Continuing education and training will not only be just something for younger persons. It will also greatly benefit the lives of older workers. Older adults will retire, only to find avenues for new work opportunities. Many will experience the joys of finding or creating new types of work. Some may even realize new talents which lay dormant during most of their earlier working years.

Rabbis, priests, and ministers/pastors will also work in their chosen professions to a later age. More second- and third-career persons are entering seminaries and the ministry today. And many faith communities are beginning to experience a shortage in leaders. Congregations will continue to see an increase in the age of its leadership, and church/synagogue leaders will find ways for continuing to maximize their calling, perhaps on a part-time or short-term basis.

Providing a sort of flex-time work schedule will increase the likelihood of older rabbis, priests, and ministers/pastors to serve congregations in some capacity. Several rabbis, priests, and ministers/pastors could serve congregations, freeing older leadership to take time off for continuing education, research, visiting family, or leisure opportunities.

4. *Older adults will provide necessary volunteer services.*

With more women entering the work force, organizations that rely heavily on volunteers will need to seek help from other ranks. Older adults are a natural resource for providing volunteer services.

Many older adults generally have more discretionary time, energy, and financial means for volunteer work. Many businesses, social services, and government-sponsored agencies today have found ways of utilizing the skills and talents of older adults. The religious community, likewise, must find ways of providing meaningful service for older adults. Folding bulletins and stuffing envelopes may be helpful volunteer services for congregations, but many older adults want to use their experience and talents in more meaningful ways.

The church and synagogue must find more aspirational and responsible roles for older persons if they are to tap into this important and valuable resource. We cannot afford to allow the wisdom, experience, and faith of our older adults to be lost or underutilized.

5. *With breakthroughs in aging research, life expectancy and longevity will continue to increase.*

"It's estimated that if some new technology could eliminate all heart disease, the average life expectancy would rise about ten years. Another five to six would be added if we could prevent all strokes, and yet another three years if cancer could be eradicated."[5]

Advances in medical technology are increasing ever more rapidly. By 2030, the over-sixty-five population will be more than one-fifth, and perhaps as high as one-fourth, of the total population.[6] At the turn of this century, persons felt blessed if they lived to sixty. By the beginning of the next century, many more Americans will live healthy, active lives in their eighties and nineties. As a result of continuing improvements in lifestyle and medical technology, today more and more people are reaching the age of one hundred and beyond.

6. Because of advances in technology, older adults will be better prepared to live independently.

Clothing, appliances, and housing will be designed for greater comfort and for maximizing the independence of older adults. With the large number of older adults, there will be an increase in the number of persons with chronic diseases. Technology will find new ways of helping persons be better able to live alone and with less dependence on the assistance of others.

Because we will be experiencing an elderculture, businesses will see the value of marketing products that sell to large numbers of older adults. In addition, with the decrease in the number of younger workers, caregiving needs will be met through other means. Older adults will expect to remain independent as long as possible and will demand that businesses and other institutions (e.g., social service agencies and church and synagogue) help them in this pursuit.

Since the American culture will shift from being focused on youth to being increasingly concerned with the needs of an older population, technology will become more "user-friendly" for older adults. Working conditions, homes, household products, buildings, and modes of transportation will all be designed to benefit older adult living.

7. The supply of family caregivers will decline as the boomer generation retires.

As indicated above, more women are joining the workforce and choosing to have fewer or no children. With the number of persons expecting to expand the ranks of the older population in the years ahead, fewer family members will be available to provide family caregiving services. If persons have enough money, the desire for this type of housing, and enough beds exist, older adults could move into nursing homes or retirement communities. Unfortunately, the price continues to escalate for nursing home beds and the cost of most retirement communities.

It is unlikely that the government will be providing the necessary funds for more low-income housing and services for the elderly. At present, the economic forecast is not good for the poor of all ages, children, and the elderly. It is quite possible, of course, that in our service-oriented economy, increasing numbers of professional care providers will emerge.

While we cannot excuse the government from its responsibility, and business will do what is financially expedient for its own behalf, the burden of caregiving will be placed more and more on the shoulders of the private sector and religious community. The private sector along with churches and synagogues will find it necessary to become more involved in caregiving. Parish nurses, social workers, certified older adult workers, and volunteer older adults themselves will need to be employed by private organizations and religious communities to meet the growing demands of an older population.

Greater commitment by the private sector along with churches and synagogues in their use of time, energy, and financial resources will be needed to care for the frail and ill older adults in our communities.

8. Many religious bodies, placing special emphasis upon ministry with children, youth, and/or young adults, will begin placing greater emphasis on ministry with adults and older adults.

By ignoring the issues and concerns facing older adults and an aging society, we will create problems for ourselves in the future. This is not an either/or situation. It is not a matter of giving our attention and financial resources to either children and youth or to older adults. We cannot afford to lose our children and youth. But neither can we afford to ignore the problems and potentials of an aging church and synagogue and a "graying" society.

We must find new ways of supporting our children, youth, and older adults. Intergenerational programming and activities that utilize the skills, wisdom, and knowledge of all generations are certainly a good start. Constructing buildings which are "user-friendly" for children and older adults is a viable use of resources. Providing day care settings to house both children and frail older adults makes a great deal of sense. Training volunteers to provide assistance in daily living needs of older adults could also be employed for families with young children.

What has become clear is this: Churches and synagogues must begin to look at the bigger picture, identify the growing needs of both children and older adults in their communities, allocate the necessary resources, and support the growing ministry to children, youth, and older adults. To do this effectively, churches and synagogues must begin to recognize a shift in paradigm from a youth-oriented culture to an elderculture.

9. Generational conflicts may arise as a result of financial, emotional, and spiritual differences.

Much talk has existed over the years about a coming war among the generations. Some experts believe this war will not take place. They believe financial resources will be available, at least until 2030, giving us time to make necessary adjustments in public policy and social programs. Others hold a different view. They predict a struggle will arise between generations as a result of financial, emotional, and spiritual differences.

Changes will take place in Social Security, Medicare, and Medicaid programs which affect large numbers of older adults. In addition, the government may make cutbacks that have a negative effect upon the financial resources of older adults in other ways. Yet, we cannot afford to put the needs of older adults and the needs of children against one another. If we do, both children and older adults will lose.

If we remain in a state of denial about the reality of an aging society, generational wars could happen and would prove difficult for everyone. If older adults are viewed as "greedy geezers," concerned only with their own well-being, the struggle will be much more intense. If we begin to plan for an aging society and face realistically the issues before us, generational conflicts may be avoided or reduced. This will require older adults to continue sharing available resources. They must view themselves and be viewed by others as givers, and not just takers. Persons working with older adults know this is true. Our society, especially many young adults, does not.

Older adults must begin to lift up the positive aspects of aging and at the same time demonstrate concern for the plight of other generations. Older adults must be willing to make sacrifices for the good of all. They must be self-giving, compassionate, and caring. Leaders and organizations that work with older adults must lead the way. The sheep need shepherds who are faithful to God and to God's commandments. Leaders must provide the vision for the people and be willing to live out the vision themselves.

Likewise, older adults must become more involved in teaching, mentoring, and modeling successful aging. Persons of every generation need the faith experience and wisdom which older adults have to offer.

10. Older adults will become more active as learning and teaching people.

Change is all around us. Many people long to go back to the "good old days." But that will not happen. "We do not need a new set of programs."[7] We have been conditioned to think programmatically about our church and synagogue life. Yet, we know that even the best programs are not working today. The answer to our frustrations is for older adults and all generations to become a teaching and learning people, just as the church and synagogue need to be teaching and learning organizations.

Problems that confront our aging congregations and society cannot be fixed by programs. "We need churches with a new consciousness of themselves and their task."[8] This is not something we can generate a program to fix. What we need is a new consciousness of ourselves as children of God so that we may rebuild the basic interaction between older adults and our social and spiritual environments. This will require that we think and act our way out of the present crisis, relying on our capacity for teaching and learning.

Peter Senge observes that "the organizations that will truly excel in the future will be organizations that discover how to tap people's commitment and capacity to learn at all levels in an organization."[9] This is equally true for older adults. The ability to solve problems and to design programs is less important than cultivating a learning attitude among an older population. Older adults themselves can model what it means to be people who learn, grow, and change, and do so successfully.

Learning opportunities abound for older adults. But mastering the game of golf or becoming a "pro" at watching TV game shows is not what we have in mind. Learning more about the will of God and sharing one's faith with other generations is vital for older adults. We cannot become too oriented to the past, complacent about the present, or too fearful about tomorrow. To do so is to become sidetracked in our task as a learning and teaching people.

Keeping our focus on the central message of Scripture and tradition is the only way to "distinguish between that which can and should be changed and that which bears the stamp of truth."[10] This means placing worship, prayer, study, faith-sharing, and service at the center of life for older adults.

We conclude with the following scenario:

> *And what of religion? The First (United) Methodist Church in a quiet middle-class neighborhood in a large city offers a vivid picture of the implications of the aging of the population for many communities. From the late 1950's through the early 1970's, its Sunday school and youth groups were overflowing, as was the playground across the street from the church on mild Saturday afternoons, when kids usually had to wait an hour for a basketball court. Now the youth groups have been consolidated and children in the Sunday school get much more individual attention than they ever did. The congregation's baby boomers are raising their own families, mostly in places scattered across the country—wherever their careers have taken them. But the church continues to play an important social role in the community: Its senior citizens' programs can barely handle the demand for activities.*[11]

Will your church or synagogue be ready to deal with these changes? Are your religious bodies comprised of leaders who are, first of all, learners and teachers?[12] Are your seminaries and divinity schools training leaders who know what it means to work with older adults? Are the older adults with whom you work interested in being learners and teachers? If you answered "No" to just one of these questions, your real work is just beginning.

Postscript

GOD'S CHALLENGE REQUIRES A NEW COMMITMENT

Good Reader:

We have come to the end of our adventure in reading together, but the real task is just beginning—and that is *the involvement of church and synagogue in effective ministry with older adults. This is none other than God's challenge, and such a challenge requires a new commitment on our part.*

We are convinced that as God's creatures, all of us are called to be God's co-creators in covenant. In other words, we are called to be God's good shepherds, ministering and witnessing to others in love, and this includes those who are aging according to God's plan. As we grow older ourselves, our task is not finished, but in a new way we are called to be "God's splendid ones" in covenantal service.

We are also convinced that the church and synagogue are called by God to be *enablers* for older persons:

- Enabling them to *serve* as well as *receive*.
- Enabling them to have *open doors for living and giving at their fullest potential.*

We sincerely hope this book has helped and will continue to help you face these challenges with a new sense of purpose and commitment.

Your friends,
Rick Gentzler and Don Clingan

Appendix A

HISTORY OF AN INTERFAITH MOVEMENT

You might say that it all began with the 1961 White House Conference on Aging, held in January of that year with 2,800 delegates in attendance. This was the first such conference on aging authorized by law and called by the President of the United States. It made a total of 947 recommendations, many of which called for public policy action.

The religious perspective or spiritual well-being of older adults was lifted up through a Committee on Religion and a significant paper written by Paul B. Maves, Ph.D., entitled "The Religious Concerns of Older Adults." However, the real inspiration on the spiritual perspective came in the final address of the conference by Abraham Heschel, professor of Jewish ethics and mysticism at the Jewish Theological Seminary of America. He spoke with a sting of truth that still has impact today. These were the words that climaxed his address (remembering that this was a time before the feminist movement):

> *Old men [and women] need a vision, not only recreation.*
> *Old men [and women] need a dream, not only a memory.*
> *It takes three things to attain a sense of significant being:*
> > *GOD,*
> > *A SOUL,*
> > *and A MOMENT.*
> *And the three are always here.*
> *Just to BE is a blessing.*
> *Just to LIVE is holy.*

The inclusion of a spiritual perspective along with the input of the Committee on Religion and Maves' 1961 paper caused the 1971 White House Conference on Aging, convened in late November, to have a whole section on spiritual well-being. Discussion for this section was based upon a background paper written by David O. Moberg, distinguished professor of sociology at Marquette University.

Of 4,000 delegates, 136 persons represented seventy-six

national religious body organizations, demonstrating the importance of religious bodies to the thinking of conference planners. The conference produced a total of 710 recommendations, including six major recommendations on "The Religious Community and the Aging," one calling for a national conference on spiritual well-being which would evaluate all conference recommendations in terms of achievements as a result of the 1971 White House Conference on Aging.

It was following this conference that the religious community took action–and for the first time in history called a National Interfaith Conference on Aging, held March 8–10, 1972, at the Christian College of Georgia in Athens. Conference chairs were Roger N. Carstensen, president of the Christian College of Georgia, and Donald F. Clingan, director of services to congregations of the National Benevolent Association of the Christian Church (Disciples of Christ). This national interfaith conference, representing Protestant, Roman Catholic, and Jewish religious bodies plus national organizations such as the National Retired Teachers Association/American Association of Retired Persons, called for the organization of a National Interfaith Coalition on Aging, Inc. (NICA).

That interfaith organization came into being the following August 1–2 in the board room of the National Center for Voluntary Action, Washington, D.C., with Donald Clingan being elected as its founding president. Other officers who served with him were Irene Sebo, O.S.B., of the U. S. Catholic Conference, vice-president for the Catholic sector; John McDowell of the National Council of Churches, vice-president for the Protestant sector; David L. Levine from the University of Georgia Council on Gerontology, vice-president for the Jewish sector; and Roger N. Carstensen, director of the secretariat.

From that time forward, the National Interfaith Coalition made a significant contribution both to the religious communities and to society as a whole in helping us to minister more effectively with older adults.

Of notable achievement were the following:

1. A Survey of Aging Programs under Religious Auspices, funded by a grant from the Administration on Aging with one hundred denominational and national religious agencies providing data.

2. Project GIST: Gerontology in Seminary Training, involving eighty seminaries and theological schools of all faiths which joined at the close of the project in an Indianapolis, Indiana, dissemination conference to share training models they had developed under the theme, "Aging, Spiritual Well-Being and Education: Innovative Models for Gerontological Training of Clergy and Lay Leaders."

3. A National Conference on Spiritual Well-Being, which did evaluate achievements in the religious community as the result of the 1971 White House Conference on Aging. Out of that conference a book entitled *Spiritual Well-Being of the Elderly* was published. This was one of the first books published on this topic. Edited by James A. Thorson, Ed.D., and Thomas C. Cook, Jr., M.A., M.Div., it was published by Charles C. Thomas, Springfield, Illinois, and copyrighted in 1980.

When the 1981 White House Conference on Aging was announced, it was obvious that the spiritual well-being of older adults would be lost in what were considered more important issues. To deal with spiritual well-being, we were told, was to violate the relationship between church and state. Therefore, there was no section on spiritual well-being and even though there were many representatives of many national religious bodies in the 1971 conference as noted before in this account, there were limited (perhaps two) delegates in the 1981 conference formally representing religious bodies (a Roman Catholic bishop and Thomas C. Cook, Jr., who then served as the executive director of the National Interfaith Coalition on Aging, were known to us). It should be noted, however, that these delegates were seen primarily as delegates from their home states.

In spite of this situation, representatives of NICA did manage to be appointed as official observers. Official observers could not be involved in the creation of recommendations as the delegates could. However, they could work with delegates who were sympathetic with the religious community and the need to address the spiritual well-being of older adults. Therefore, despite the lack of formal delegates, NICA was able to influence the passing of forty-five recommendations which dealt with some element of spiritual well-being, these forty-five being out of a total of 668.

Parenthetically, before the 1981 White House Conference, the secretary of health and human services was given the responsibility of appointing sixteen technical committees, one of these committees being on the theme of "An Age Integrated Society: Implications for Spiritual Well-Being." Although this committee met strictly *before* the White House Conference, the religious sector was able to have some impact on the conference itself by sharing this committee's written report.

Beyond 1981, the National Interfaith Coalition continued to move forward in its services to the religious sector and society as a whole. It served as a co-sponsor of the Robert Wood Johnson Foundation's Interfaith Volunteer Caregivers Program and also conducted biennial conferences on such subjects as "Concerns about Dying" and "Aging and the Human Spirit," the latter being co-sponsored with the American Society on Aging Forum on Religion and Aging.

In January 1991 NICA became a constituent unit of the National Council on the Aging, Inc. This strengthened NICA's membership and financial base and gave it greater ability to address public policy. It also provided the means to secure grants for projects that would enable the religious sector to be more effective in ministry with older adults at all levels.

The National Clergy Leadership Project to Prepare for an Aging Society, funded by a grant from the Administration on Aging, is an example of such a project. It consists of a video, a magazine of articles on issues of aging, a leader manual, and a resource manual written for an interfaith audience.

When the 1995 White House Conference on Aging was called by President Bill Clinton, immediately representatives of the "National Four" (organizations existing in the field of religion, spirituality and aging) met to register their feelings about the importance of the spiritual perspective and the spiritual well-being of older adults as a part of the conference agenda. The National Four included:

1. **The National Interfaith Coalition on Aging, a unit of the National Council on the Aging, Inc.,**
2. **The American Society on Aging Forum on Religion, Spirituality, and Aging,**

3. **Shepherd's Centers of America, and**
4. **The National Federation of Interfaith Volunteer Caregivers, Inc.**

Besides National Four communications, the board members of these organizations were encouraged to write letters to the 1995 White House conference policy committee, the executive director of the White House Conference, Robert B. Blancato, and President Clinton to register our joint feelings about issues that needed to be included in the conference agenda that would address the spiritual well-being of older adults.

Among the responses received, Thomas H. D. Mahoney, a member of the conference structure working group of the conference policy committee, informed Donald Clingan that "under the Quality of Life Issue to be discussed at the Conference, an important sub-issue will be Spiritual Well-Being as well as Ethics and Values."

As in 1981, again in 1995, out of 2,217 delegates (including for the first time twenty youth delegates), a limited number of delegates formally representing national religious bodies were appointed. (In fact, we know of only one, this one being appointed from the national offices of the Salvation Army.) If religious body delegates existed, they primarily had to be delegates from their home state by appointment of their governor or their U. S. representatives or senators.

The conference theme was "America Now and into the 21st Century: Generations Aging Together with Independence, Opportunity, and Dignity." Meeting May 2–5, 1995, in Washington D.C., the delegates were joined by three hundred official observers, thirty-five international observers, five hundred volunteers, and two hundred and fifty members of the press from across the country to discuss America's aging policies and programs. *The 1995 White House Conference on Aging was the last of its kind to be held in the twentieth century and the first to face the challenges of the twenty-first century.*

As the conference began, the delegates were involved in an opening speak-out which provided, in an organized fashion, an informal means of voicing their opinions without the restrictions of parliamentary procedure. This was followed by presentations from many key figures in the existing administration (including the president, vice-president, and first lady, along with the top cabinet officials concerned for older adults). Bipartisan representatives from the U. S. Congress also made presentations, along with key figures in the general field of aging.

The three working sessions of the conference divided the delegates into small issue resolution development sessions (IRDS) of about fifty persons each in which they discussed and modified conference draft resolutions. These resolutions were crafted by the White House Conference policy and advisory committees after they reviewed recommendations from some eight hundred pre-conference events (including some sixteen to twenty mini-conferences on spiritual well-being) and then shared with the delegates for study previous to the formal conference itself. The draft resolutions belonged to four main issue categories:

1. Assuring comprehensive health care including long-term care.
2. Promoting economic security.
3. Maximizing housing and support service options.
4. Maximizing options for a quality of life.

It was under the latter category that two draft resolutions were considered under the heading of "Spiritual Well-Being, Ethics, Values and Roles," these being "Encouraging Development and Ensuring Implementation of Advance Directives" and "Meeting the Spiritual Needs of Older Persons." Attempts were made to strengthen particularly the latter, but to little avail. The result was that it was *not* adopted in the final vote by the conference among its top forty priorities.

After the IRDS sessions, during the last night of the conference, a steering committee composed of members of the White House Conference policy and advisory committees consolidated the modifications to the draft resolutions made during the IRDS and presented the final resolutions to the delegates for a vote.

In addition to the draft resolutions, a delegate could introduce his or her own resolution and submit it for consideration at the final vote, provided the resolution was supported with the signatures of at least ten percent of the total number of delegates. In the final vote (much different from previous conferences and certainly more workable as they prepared a final report for use by the Clinton

Administration and the Congress and other appropriate governmental bodies on state, county, and city level), the delegates were asked to vote for forty of the resolutions developed in the IRDS and for as many of the thirty-nine delegate-introduced resolutions as they wished.

The final fifty adopted resolutions plus one more discovered later to have sufficient votes are printed by title and number of votes in Appendix B of this book. The implications of the 1995 White House Conference on Aging in addressing the issues associated with the spiritual well-being of older adults is recorded in the final chapter of this book on "Challenges of the Future."

Appendix B

RESOLUTIONS ADOPTED BY THE 1995 WHITE HOUSE CONFERENCE ON AGING

# of Votes*	Resolution Title /(Resolution #)
1597	Keeping Social Security Sound for Now and for the Future (7.1)
1573	Preserving the Integrity of the Older Americans Act (4.7)
1427	Preserving the Nature of Medicaid (4.2)
1406	Ensuring the Future of the Medicare Program (4.1)
1379	Ensuring the Availability of a Broad Spectrum of Services (3.1)
1376	Preserving Advocacy Functions under the Older Americans Act (4.8)
1371	Financing and Providing Long-Term Care and Services (3.2)
1365	Acknowledging the Contribution of Older Volunteers (20.1)
1322	Assuming Personal Responsibility for the State of One's Health (1.1)
1296	Strengthening the Federal Role in Building and Sustaining a Well-Trained Work Force Grounded in Geriatric and Gerontological Education (5.3)
1292	Expanding, Coordinating, and Targeting Necessary Services (16.1)
1288	Reforming the Health Care System (2.4)
1258	Promoting Innovative Strategies to Encourage new Models of Supportive Housing, Particularly Housing Which Facilitates Long-term Care Services (14.2)
1240	Expanding the Coverage of Existing Food Programs (9.1)
1195	Preventing Crimes Against Older Persons (17.1)
1190	Prevention/Wellness Throughout One's Lifespan (1.2)
1190	Preventing Elder Abuse, Exploitation and Neglect (17.2)
1172	Expanding Training and Employment Opportunities for Older Workers (6.2)
1171	Designing Housing to Maximize Independence (12.1)
1170	Providing Services in a Full Range of Locations that Encompasses: Institutional Care; Home Care/Foster Home Care; Community-Based Services (4.4)
1162	Increasing Federal Funding for Research in the Areas of the Mechanisms of Aging, Diseases of Older People, Long-Term Care, Systems and Services Research, and Special Populations (5.1)

1157	Developing Alternative Options for Funding Long-Term Care (4.6)
1145	Providing Oversight and Ensuring Pension Solvency, Portability, and Earlier Vestment (8.1)
1129	Setting Ground Rules for Guardianship (22.1)
1126	Support for Caregivers (3.3)
1120	Enhancing Community Participation (21.1)
1117	Maximizing Transportation Choices (15.3)
1110	Ensuring the Availability of Appropriate Care, Services, and Treatment (2.3)
1110	Expanding Federal and State Housing Programs (13.1)
1093	Encouraging Policies that Support and Reward the Development of Suitable and Safe Communities (14.1)
1080	Providing Health Care Coverage that Addresses Basic Needs, Prevention, and Chronic Disease Concerns (4.3)
1042	Ensuring Quality Care, Services and Treatment (2.2)
1037	Meeting Mental Health Needs (21.2)
1036	Promoting Positive Images of Aging by Sensitizing Society to the Value of Older Adults (19.1)
1034	Expanding Programs to Assess and Address Malnutrition (9.3)
1022	Addressing Issues Related to Grandparents Raising Grandchildren (20.3)
1022	Targeting Social Security Benefits for Frail Elderly Women (7.3)
1011	Enforcing Laws Against Age Discrimination (11.1)
1007	Encouraging Development and Ensuring Implementation of Advance Directives (18.1)

*–out of a possible 1988 votes

Adopted Resolutions Introduced by Delegates

# of Votes*	Resolution Title/(Resolution #)
1414	Reauthorization of the Older Americans Act (121)
1413	Alzheimer Research (70)
1217	Meeting Mental Health Needs (65)
1212	Long-Term Care Financing (82)
1186	Social Security/Entitlements (78)
1181	Protecting Medicare and Medicaid (145)
1156	Comprehensive Health Care (77)
1106	Need to Preserve and Expand Elderly Housing (80)
1080	Legal Assistance (83)
1043	Income Security (79)

*–out of a possible 1907 votes

Appendix C

FACTS ABOUT AGING: A QUIZ

(True or False)

T F

□ □ 1. One in eight Americans are sixty-five years of age and older.

□ □ 2. Older adults depend more heavily on investments and private pension programs for their income than they do on any other source.

□ □ 3. As people grow older, they become more alike.

□ □ 4. By the year 2030, there will be proportionately more older adults than children and youth in the population.

□ □ 5. Women age sixty-five years and older outnumber older men by three to two.

□ □ 6. The majority of older adults would rather continue at least some kind of paid part-time work after retirement.

□ □ 7. Older adults who live alone have higher incomes than older couples.

□ □ 8. Older adults tend to view their health negatively.

□ □ 9. Alzheimer's disease is the leading cause of cognitive impairment in older adults.

□ □ 10. Approximately seventeen percent of older adults live in nursing homes.

□ □ 11. Because of better health care and nutrition, the number of nursing home residents will probably decrease in the future.

□ □ 12. As people grow older, their ability to learn decreases.

□ □ 13. Arthritis is the leading chronic illness of persons age sixty-five and older.

□ □ 14. Approximately two out of every three older adults live in a family setting.

□ □ 15. Older men are more likely to live alone than older women.

□ □ 16. In 1990, the U.S. ranked in the top five countries in terms of life expectancy.

□ □ 17. The percentage of older men in the labor force has declined rapidly over the last forty years.

Appendix D

FACTS ABOUT AGING: ANSWERS

1. TRUE: According to the U.S. Bureau of the Census, persons age sixty-five years of age and older comprised 12.5 percent of the total U.S. population in 1990.
2. FALSE: Older adults depend more heavily on Social Security for their income than they do on any other source.
3. FALSE: Older adults are probably the least homogeneous group of all age groups. They have had a variety of life experiences. Over the years they have had different educational opportunities, work experiences, and assorted losses. They have experienced life's many changes and have come from a variety of cultural and religious backgrounds.
4. TRUE: The U.S. Bureau of Census projects that persons age sixty-five years and older will make up twenty-two percent and children and youth will make up twenty percent of U.S. population.
5. TRUE: The U.S. Bureau of Census indicates that there are over eighteen million women and only thirteen million men.
6. TRUE: According to a nationwide poll by Lou Harris, about three-quarters of the labor force would rather continue some kind of paid part-time work after retirement.
7. FALSE: Older married couples have a higher level of income than older adults living alone.
8. FALSE: Recent studies indicate that more than seventy percent of older adults indicate that their health is excellent, very good, or good—while less than thirty percent said fair or poor.
9. TRUE: According to recent studies, Alzheimer's disease affects more than four million Americans.
10. FALSE: While the rate of nursing home use by older adults has doubled since the introduction of Medicare and Medicaid in 1966, it is only 2.5 to 5 percent of the population age sixty-five years of age and older.
11. FALSE: On the contrary, because of the increase in older adult population, especially among persons eighty-five years and older, the number of nursing home residents will continue to increase.

12. FALSE: Studies show that older adults are capable of learning new things. While older persons can learn as well as younger persons, they learn differently.
13. TRUE: According to the National Center for Health Statistics, arthritis is the leading chronic illness, followed by hypertension, hearing impairment, heart disease, cataracts, deformity/orthopedic, chronic sinusitis, and diabetes.
14. TRUE: According to the U.S. Bureau of Census, thirty-one percent of the persons age sixty-five years and older live alone; fifty-four percent are married and live with spouses; and the remaining fifteen percent reside with others—including children, relatives, or friends.
15. FALSE: Older women are more likely to live alone and older men are more likely to live with a spouse.
16. FALSE: Some countries that rank ahead of the U.S. include: Canada, France, Italy, Germany, Japan, Sweden, and United Kingdom.
17. TRUE: According to the U.S. Bureau of Census, in 1950, forty-six percent of all men age sixty-five years and older were in the labor force. This figure dropped to thirty-three percent by 1960, to twenty-seven percent by 1970, and to seventeen percent by 1989.

Appendix E

NEEDS AND TALENTS SURVEY FORM

Before using this survey form, the local church volunteer should:
1. Contact the person to be interviewed and establish a mutually-agreed-upon day and time for the interview.
2. Upon arriving for the interview, identify yourself and briefly state the nature of your visit.
3. Give the person being interviewed a copy of this survey form, read each question aloud, and record the information on your form.

NAME _____

ADDRESS_____

TELEPHONE _____

INTERVIEWER _____ DATE _____

1. Marital Status
    ❑ Single   ❑ Married   ❑ Separated
    ❑ Widowed   ❑ Divorced

2. Sex
    ❑ Male   ❑ Female

3. Birthdate _____

4. Do you live alone?
    ❑ Yes   ❑ No   With Whom?_____

5. In an emergency, is there someone to whom you could turn for assistance?
    ❑ No   ❑ Yes
    Whom? _____

6. During this past week, how many times did you:
Have someone come to visit with you? _____
Talk with a friend or relative on the telephone? _____
Go visit someone else? _____

7. How do you rate your overall health?
❏ Excellent   ❏ Very good
❏ Good   ❏ Fair
❏ Poor

8. What problems do you experience where you live?
_____
_____

9. What is/was your occupation? _____

10. Transportation
I need transportation to:
❏ Church/synagogue   ❏ Doctor's office
❏ Health clinic   ❏ Shopping
Other _____
I could help transport others to _____

11. Minor Home Repair and Maintenance Service
I need help with:
❏ Plumbing   ❏ Moving items
❏ Painting   ❏ Lawn care
❏ Carpentry
Other _____
I could help others with home repairs _____

12. Home Chore Service
I need help with:
❏ Sewing   ❏ Cooking
❏ Cleaning   ❏ Laundry
❏ Writing letters ❏ Other
I could help others with home chores_____

13. Health Care

I need help with:
- ❏ Medical care ❏ Dental care
- ❏ Vision care ❏ Hearing loss
- ❏ Nutrition

Other _____

I could help others with health care _____

14. Legal and Financial Counsel

I need help with:
- ❏ Will planning ❏ Medicare or Medicaid
- ❏ Social Security ❏ Insurance

Other _____

I could help others with legal/financial advice _____

15. Religious Services

I Need:
- ❏ Clergy visitation ❏ lay visitation
- ❏ Devotional materials ❏ Other

I could help others with religious services _____

16. Personal Contacts

I need:
- ❏ Daily telephone calls ❏ Friendly visits
- ❏ Cards and letters from congregation members

Other _____

I could help others with personal contacts_____

17. Social, educational , and recreational programs

I'm interested in:
- ❏ Travel ❏ Group games
- ❏ Exercise/fitness classes ❏ Fellowship classes
- ❏ Reading ❏ Audio books
- ❏ Videos ❏ G.E.D. classes
- ❏ Other_____

I could help others with _____

Appendix F

OLDER ADULT MINISTRY REVIEW
FOR CHURCH AND SYNAGOGUE

1. **Church/Synagogue Name** _____

2. **What is the total membership of your church or synagogue?**

3. **What is the total number of persons age sixty-five years and older in your church or synagogue?** _____

4. **What is the percentage of total membership of persons age sixty-five years and older?** _____

5. **Do you have an Older Adult Council or another organization responsible for older adult ministries? (Name)** __
   _____

6. **Indicate the numbers of older adults who are:**
   ❑ Homebound _____
   ❑ Residents of nursing homes and retirement centers _____
   ❑ Active in your local church or synagogue _____
   ❑ Living out-of-town or out-of-state _____
   ❑ Other (please specify) _____

7. **State your church or synagogues mission, vision, or aim for older adult ministries.**
   _____
   _____
   _____
   _____

8. **Does your church or synagogue provide a ministry to older adults living in your community but who are not members or regular attenders of your church or synagogue?**
   ❑ Yes
   ❑ No

9. **Do you have a list of older adult volunteers who visit church or synagogue members who are:**
   ❑ In the hospital?
   ❑ In nursing homes or retirement centers?
   ❑ Homebound?
   ❑ In prison?

10. **Are older adults represented on the official or administrative board or other governing body of your church or synagogue?** _____
    ❑ Yes
    ❑ No

11. **Does your church or synagogue provide any of the following forms of ministry?**
    ❑ Transportation to worship, fellowship activities, Bible study, doctor's office, shopping
    ❑ Other _____
    ❑ Adult day care
    ❑ Meals-on-Wheels
    ❑ Sponsor a Shepherd's Center
    ❑ Tape ministry: audio and/or video tape of worship and special activities for homebound, nursing home residents and others
    ❑ Minor home maintenance and repair service
    ❑ Home chore service
    ❑ Parish nurse program
    ❑ Social worker program
    ❑ Respite care relievers program
    ❑ Stephen Ministry
    ❑ Volunteer in mission program
    ❑ Fitness, exercise, and nutrition classes
    ❑ Telephone reassurance program
    ❑ Prayer/concern chains
    ❑ Emergency hotline
    ❑ Support groups: widow-to-widow program, stroke support group, caregivers support group, etc.
    ❑ Older adult banquet and program
    ❑ Special worship services for homebound
    ❑ Special work mission trips

❑ Special fellowship trips
❑ Special educational trips and tours
❑ Tax preparation
❑ Other (please specify) _____

12. Does your church offer the following classes or seminars for older adults?

❑ Grief and loss
❑ Faith development
❑ Financial planning
❑ Death and dying
❑ Marriage enrichment
❑ Caregiving
❑ Other (please specify) _____

13. Do older adults in your local church or synagogue participate as teachers/leaders in any of the following teaching ministries?

❑ For children
❑ For youth
❑ For young adults
❑ For middle adults
❑ For older adults

14. Do older adults in your local church or synagogue participate as leaders in any of the following intergenerational activities:

❑ After-school program for children
❑ Children's telephone reassurance program
❑ Children's day care or preschool program
❑ Scouting activities
❑ Confirmation, Bar Mitzvah, or other faith mentoring
❑ Classes for children or youth
❑ Puppet or clown ministry
❑ Camping or retreat programs
❑ Special study classes
❑ Other (please specify) _____

15. **Do older adults in your local church or synagogue serve in any of the following ways?**
    - ❏ Greeters
    - ❏ Ushers
    - ❏ Liturgists or lay readers
    - ❏ Song leaders
    - ❏ Soloists/choir members/cantors
    - ❏ Church/synagogue office assistance
    - ❏ Church/synagogue food and clothing assistance program
    - ❏ Other (please specify) _____

16. **What is the dollar amount your church or synagogu has budgeted for older adult ministries this year?**

    Administrative and staff costs _____

    Mission and outreach _____

    Publicity and marketing _____

    Other (please specify) _____

17. **Have you received any federal, state, or private grant-funding for your older adult ministries program?**

    If yes, how much? _____

    Source of grant _____

    Purpose of grant _____

18. **What other areas of ministry by, with, and for older adults would you like your church or synagogue to be involved in?**

    _____
    _____
    _____
    _____

Appendix G

CHURCH-SYNAGOGUE ACCESSIBILITY SURVEY
(Yes Or No)

1. Church or synagogue entrance and halls
Y N
- ❏ ❏ Is there a ramp or level entrance to your church or synagogue door which can be used by persons with disabilities?
- ❏ ❏ Is there a directory and/or directional signs so people know where to go upon arrival?
- ❏ ❏ Are Braille signs utilized and placed between 4'6" to 5'6" from floor?
- ❏ ❏ Are there handrails at the church or synagogue entrance?
- ❏ ❏ Are there handrails in the hallways?

2. Parking
- ❏ ❏ Are there parking spaces marked "Handicapped Parking"?
- ❏ ❏ Is the parking lot well lighted at night?
- ❏ ❏ Is there a level approach to the church or synagogue from parking area or the street?

3. Restrooms
- ❏ ❏ Are there handrails in the washrooms and toilets?
- ❏ ❏ Are restrooms wheelchair-accessible?
- ❏ ❏ Are restrooms accessible to sanctuary?
- ❏ ❏ Are restrooms accessible to classrooms and meeting rooms?
- ❏ ❏ Are restrooms accessible to social or fellowship hall?
- ❏ ❏ Do restrooms have a cot or sofa for persons needing to lie down?

4. Sanctuary
- ❏ ❏ Can your sanctuary accommodate wheelchairs?
- ❏ ❏ Is there adequate lighting on speaker's face to facilitate speech reading?

Y N

❑ ❑ Is there adequate lighting for reading in all pews?

❑ ❑ Are large-print Bibles, hymnals, and other worship materials available?

❑ ❑ Does your sound system provide adequate transmission without dead spots?

❑ ❑ Are there individual hearing devices for the hearing impaired?

❑ ❑ Are pews cushioned for added comfort?

❑ ❑ Is there a temperature-controlled heating and cooling system?

❑ ❑ Are guide dogs permitted in your church or synagogue sanctuary?

5. Doors

❑ ❑ Do doors swing without conflict to wheelchairs?

❑ ❑ Are there vertical door handles or horizontal door bars, rather than slippery round knobs?

6. Elevators

❑ ❑ Are buttons in elevator low enough for wheelchair reach?

❑ ❑ Are Braille signs used with each elevator button?

7. Programs

❑ ❑ Are programs and meetings arranged at times suitable for older adults?

❑ ❑ Are the resources and materials used suitable for the needs of older adults?

8. Transportation

❑ ❑ For persons who cannot use public transportation and do not have private cars or vans, does the church/synagogue have volunteer drivers and vehicles which are available for church/synagogue activities?

❑ ❑ Does the church/synagogue have a van capable of transporting persons in wheelchairs (i.e., with ramps or lifts and clamps for wheelchairs)?

9. Worship, Sunday or Sabbath school, and administrative functions.

Are older adults invited and encouraged to participate as:

Y   N

☐ ☐ Greeters

☐ ☐ Ushers

☐ ☐ Liturgists or lay readers

☐ ☐ Choir members or soloists/cantors

☐ ☐ Sunday or Sabbath school teachers

☐ ☐ Class officers or leaders

☐ ☐ Committee members

☐ ☐ Church or synagogue administrative officers

10. Additional comments:

_____

_____

_____

_____

After the Older Adult Council reviews this survey, you will want to address deficiencies with your minister, pastor, priest, or rabbi. Plan to meet with your official board or other governing body and develop a plan of action for making improvements.

Appendix H

RANGE OF COMMUNITY SERVICES AND OPPORTUNITIES FOR OLDER ADULTS

A range of services and opportunities to meet various aspects of dependent living as they occur during later adulthood, with the associated objective of maintaining the optimum degree of independent living.

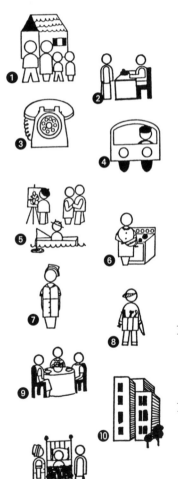

1. Independent living in own home

2. Information, Counseling and Referral Services

3. Visitation Services
   • Telephone reassurance
   • In-person visitation

4. Transportation Services

5. Community Activity Programs

6. Homemaker Services

7. Home Health Care Services

8. Home Repair Services

9. Foster/Day Care Services

10. Retirement Services
    • Apartment living
    • Hotel-like living
    • Congregate living

11. Nursing Home Services
    • Personal or intermediate care
    • Skilled care
    • Long-term care

Appendix I

Community Social Service Agency Survey

Name of Agency _____

Date _____

Address _____

_____

Telephone _____

Contact Person _____

Position _____

(Attach any brochures or other promotional materials distributed by this agency)

1. **Purpose and function of the agency** _____

_____

_____

2. **Services provided for older adults** _____

_____

_____

3. **Eligibility requirements for participating older adults**

_____

_____

4. **Costs for participants** _____

5. **Number of older adults served by the agency** _____

6. Are present facilities adequate for its program? _____

7. Are older adult volunteers used? ❑ **Yes** ❑ **No**
If *Yes*, how are they used? _____

_____

_____

8. What unmet needs of older adults has the agency discovered?

_____

_____

_____

9. Does the agency have plans to meet these unmet needs?
   ❑ **Yes** ❑ **No**
If *Yes*, when? _____
How will these unmet needs be met? _____

_____

_____

10. What can your church or synagogue do to assist the
agency in its program? _____

_____

_____

List other observations and comments on the back of this form.

Appendix J

COMMUNITY SERVICE ORGANIZATION
POTENTIAL FOR OLDER ADULT PROGRAMS

1. **Economic Organizations**
   - *Corporations*
   - *Chamber of Commerce*
   - *Vocation groups*
   Unions
   Retail merchants association
   Farmers association
   Boards of banks, corporations
   Professional associations

2. **Government Organizations**
   - *Federal departments and agencies*
   Local offices: General Services Administration, Equal
   Employment Opportunity Commission, Department of
   Health and Human Services, etc.
   - *State departments and agencies*
   Local offices: Bureau of Vocational Rehabilitation, Health
   Department, Welfare Department, etc.
   - *County departments and agencies*
   Local offices: Aid for the aged, Cooperative Extension,
   Welfare Department, etc.
   - *Community departments and agencies*
   Recreation Department, Welfare Department, Health
   Department, Housing Division, Board of Education, etc.

3. **Education Organizations**
   - Better school groups
   - Parent-teacher organizations
   - Adult education groups

4. **Religious Organizations**
   - Churches and synagogues
   - Groups associated with churches and synagogues

- Ecumenical organizations, commissions
- Clergy associations
- Laity associations
- Primarily religious (Bible study groups, worship groups)
- Other (clubs, teams, social groups)

5. **Cultural, Fraternal, and Recreational Organizations**
   - Concert societies
   - Study and forum groups
   - Art societies
   - Dramatic groups
   - Literary societies
   - Nationality group fraternal associations
   - Occupation-oriented fraternal associations (police leagues)
   - Other fraternities, lodges, granges, secret societies
   - Athletic teams
   - Athletic clubs
   - Hobby clubs
   - Social enjoyment groups
   - Groups serving one particular minority

6. **Civic Organizations**
   - Service clubs
   - Good government leagues
   - Patriotic and veterans associations
   - Taxpayers associations
   - Political party organizations
   - Neighborhood planning associations
   - Real estate associations
   - Housing associations

7. **Health and Welfare Organizations**
   - Charitable organizations
   - Religious charitable organizations
   - Boards of social agencies
   - Welfare or humane associations
   - Child welfare organizations
   - Youth organizations
   - Federations of professional workers
   - Organizations of particular diseases (heart, cancer, arthritis)

- General community health groups
- Safety council

8. Community and Planning Organizations
- United community service organizations
- Chests, united funds, councils
- Community action agencies (poverty)
- Community planning associations
- Coordinating committees
- Federations of clubs
- Other intergroup agencies or organizations

9. Specific Community Resources for Older Adult Programs
Look in your local "Yellow Pages" under social service organizations for addresses and telephone number of such organizations as:
- AFL-CIO Community Service
- ACTION (R.S.V.P.)
- Area agencies on aging
- Catholic Social Service
- Community action program
- Community service council
- Community mental health agency
- Community college
- Council of churches
- Family Service Association
- Foster Grandparent Program
- Home health care agency
- Homemaker service
- Information and referral service
- Jewish Community Center
- Jewish Family Service
- Legal service organization
- Meals on Wheels
- Title VII Nutrition Program
- Park and recreation department
- Public housing authority
- Public library
- Salvation Army
- Senior citizens center
- Settlement center

- Social Security Administration
- UAW Community Service
- University
- Urban League
- Visiting Nurses Association
- YMCA and YWCA

Appendix K

A SELECT LIST OF NATIONAL AND INTERNATIONAL ORGANIZATIONS IN THE FIELD OF AGING

ACTION
1100 Vermont Avenue, N.W.
Washington, DC 20525
ACTION includes:
Foster Grandparent Program (FGP)
Senior Companion Program (SCP)
Retired Senior Volunteer Program (RSVP)
Volunteers in Service to America (VISTA)

ALZHEIMER'S DISEASE AND RELATED DISORDERS ASSOC. INC.
919 N. Michigan Avenue, Suite 1000
Chicago, IL 60611-1676

AMERICAN ASSOCIATION OF HOMES AND SERVICES FOR THE AGING
901 E Street, N.W., Suite 500
Washington, DC 20004-2837

AMERICAN ASSOCIATION OF RETIRED PERSONS
601 E Street, N.W.
Washington, DC 20049

AMERICAN HEALTH CARE ASSOCIATION
1201 L Street, N.W.
Washington, DC 20005

AMERICAN INDIAN HEALTH CARE ASSOCIATION
245 East 6th Street, Suite 499
St. Paul, MN 55101-1918

AMERICAN JEWISH CONGRESS
15 East 84th Street
New York, NY 10026

AMERICAN SOCIETY ON AGING
833 Market Street, Suite 512
San Francisco, CA 94103
Includes the Forum on Religion, Spirituality and Aging

B'NAI B'RITH INTERNATIONAL
1640 Rhode Island Avenue, N.W.
Washington, DC 20036

CATHOLIC GOLDEN AGE
430 Penn Avenue
Scranton, PA 18503

COUNCIL OF JEWISH FEDERATIONS
730 Broadway
New York, NY 10003

ELDERHOSTEL
75 Federal Street
Boston, MA 02110

GERONTOLOGICAL SOCIETY OF AMERICA
1275 K Street, N.W., Suite 350
Washington, DC 20005-4006

GRAY PANTHERS
2025 Pennsylvania Avenue, N.W.,
Suite 821
Washington, DC 20006

**HISPANIC AMERICAN
GERIATRICS SOCIETY**
1 Cutts Road
Durham, NH 03824-3102

**INTERNATIONAL FEDERATION
ON AGEING**
Publications Division
601 E Street, N.W.
Washington, DC 20049

**INTERNATIONAL SOCIETY FOR
RETIREMENT PLANNING**
11312 Old Club Road
Rockville, MD 20852

**NATIONAL ASIAN PACIFIC
RESOURCE CENTER ON AGING**
Melbourne Tower
1511 Third Avenue, Suite 914
Seattle, WA 98101

**NATIONAL ASSOCIATION FOR
HISPANIC ELDERLY**
3325 Wilshire Blvd., Suite 800
Los Angeles, CA 90010-1724

**NATIONAL ASSOCIATION OF
AREA AGENCIES ON AGING**
1112-16th Street, N.W., Suite 100
Washington, DC 20036

**NATIONAL ASSOCIATION OF
STATE UNITS ON AGING**
1224 Eye Street, N.W., Suite 725
Washington, DC 20005

**NATIONAL BLACK AGING
NETWORK**
1212 Broadway, Suite 830
Oakland, CA 94612

**NATIONAL CAUCUS AND
CENTER ON BLACK AGED**
1424 K Street, N.W., Suite 500
Washington, DC 20005

**NATIONAL COUNCIL OF
SENIOR CITIZENS**
1331 F Street, N.W.
Washington, DC 20004-1171

**NATIONAL COUNCIL
ON THE AGING, INC.**
409 3rd Street, S.W.
Washington, DC 20024
*This is also the address for the following
constituent units of the National Council
on the Aging:*

*The National Interfaith Coalition on
Aging (NICA)*

The Health Promotion Institute (HPI)

*The National Adult Day Services
Association (NADSA)*

*The National Association of Older Worker
Employment Services (NAOWES)*

*The National Center for Voluntary
Leadership in Aging (NCVLA)*

*The National Center on Rural Aging
(NCRA)*

*The National Institute of Senior Centers
(NISC)*

*The National Institute of Senior Housing
(NISH)*

*The National Institute on Community-
based Long-term Care (NICLC)*

*The National Institute on Financial Issues
and Services for Elders (NIFSE)*

*The National Voluntary Organizations for
Independent Living for the Aging
(NVOILA)*

**NATIONAL FEDERATION OF
INTERFAITH VOLUNTEER
CAREGIVERS**
368 Broadway, Suite 103
Kingston, NY 12401

**NATIONAL HISPANIC
COUNCIL ON AGING**
2713 Ontario Road, N.W.
Washington, DC 20009

**NATIONAL HOSPICE
ORGANIZATION**
1901 North Moore Street, Suite 901
Arlington, VA 22209

**NATIONAL INDIAN
COUNCIL ON AGING**
6400 Uptown Blvd., N.E., Suite 501W
Albuquerque, NM 87110

**NORTH AMERICAN ASSOCIA-
TION OF JEWISH HOMES AND
HOUSING FOR THE AGING**
10830 North Central Expressway,
Suite 150
Dallas, TX 75231-1022

OLDER WOMEN'S LEAGUE
666 11th Street N.W., Suite 700
Washington, DC 20001

**SOCIAL SECURITY
ADMINISTRATION**
6401 Security Boulevard
Baltimore, MD 21235

**U. S. CONGRESS SENATE
SPECIAL COMMITTEE ON AGING**
G-31 Dirksen Building
Washington, DC 20510-6400

**DEPARTMENT OF
VETERANS AFFAIRS**
810 Vermont Avenue, N.W.
Washington, DC 20420

Appendix L

OFFICES OF THE ADMINISTRATION ON AGING

**THE ADMINISTRATION
ON AGING**
Wilbur J. Cohen Building
330 Independence Avenue, S.W.
Washington, DC 20201
Phone: (202) 619-0011

REGIONAL OFFICES
REGION 1 (CT, ME, NH, RI, VT)
J. F. Kennedy Federal Building
Government Center, Room 2007
Boston, MA 02203
Phone: (617) 565-1158

**REGION 2 (NJ, NY,
Puerto Rico, Virgin Islands)**
Javitz Federal Building, Room 38-102
26 Federal Plaza
New York, NY 10278
Phone: (212) 264-2976

REGION 3 (DE, MD, PA, VA, WV)
Gateway Building
3535 Market Street
P. O. Box 13716
Philadelphia, PA 19101
Phone: (215) 596-6891

**REGION 4 (AL, FL, GA, KY,
MS, NC, SC, TN)**
101 Marietta Tower, Suite 1702
Atlanta, GA 30323
Phone: (404) 331-5900

**REGION 5 (IL, IN, MI, MN, OH,
WI)**
105 West Adams Street, 20th Floor
Chicago, IL 60603
Phone: (312) 353-3141

REGION 6 (AR, LA, NM, OK, TX)
1200 Main Tower Building,
Room 1000
Dallas, TX 75202
Phone: (214) 767-2971

REGION 7 (IA, KS, MO, NE)
1150 Grand Avenue, Suite 600
Kansas City, MO 64106
Phone: (816) 374-6015

REGION 8 (CO, MT, ND, SD, UT, WY)
1961 Stout Street, Room 308
Denver, CO 80294
Phone: (303) 844-2951

**REGION 9 (AZ, CA, HI, NV,
American Samoa, Guam, Trust
Territory)**
50 U. N. Plaza, Room 480
San Francisco, CA 94102
Phone: (415) 556-6003

REGION 10 (AK, ID, OR, WA)
Blanchard Plaza Building, RX-33,
Room 1200
2201 6th Avenue
Seattle, WA 98121
Phone: (206) 615-2298

*STATE OFFICES/AREA AGENCIES
ON AGING*
State offices and area agencies on
aging are a part of the aging network
and may be contacted for helpful
information on programs, technical
assistance, and resource materials relative to older adults.

157

SELECTED PRINT AND AUDIOVISUAL RESOURCES—BOOKS (b) AND VIDEOS (v)

CAREGIVING AND AGING PARENTS

Adams, Tom and Kathryn Armstrong. *When Parents Age: What Children Can Do.* New York: Berkley Books, 1993. (b)

A Good Place to Grow Old. San Francisco, Calif.: American Society on Aging. 32 min. (v)

Andresen, Gayle. *Caring for People with Alzheimer's Disease: A Training Manual for Direct Care Providers.* Baltimore, Md.: Health Professions Press, 1995. (b)

Ball, Avis Jane. *Caring for an Aging Parent.* Buffalo, N.Y.: Prometheus Books. 1986. (b)

Caro, Francis G. and Arthur E. Blank. *Quality Impact of Home Care for the Elderly.* Binghamton, N.Y.: The Haworth Press, Inc., 1989. (b)

Campbell, James. *What Do You Say?* Nashville, Tenn.: Discipleship Resources, 1991. (b)

Deedy, John. *Your Aging Parents.* Chicago, Ill.: The Thomas Moore Press, 1984. (b)

Gallagher, Sally K. *Older People Giving Care: Helping Family and Community.* Westport, Ct.: Auburn House, 1994. (b)

Hooyman, Nancy R. and Wendy Lustbader. *Taking Care of Your Aging Family Members.* New York: The Free Press, A Division of Macmillan, Inc. 1988. (b)

In Care of: Families and Their Elders. New York: The Brookdale Center on the Aging, Hunter College, 1988. 55 min. (v)

Kane, Rosalie A. And Joan D. Penrod, *Family Caregiving in an Aging Society: Policy Perspectives.* Newbury Park, Calif.: SAGE Publications, Inc., 1995. (b)

Memories of Love: Caring for the Caregiver. Silver Spring, Md.: Alzheimer's Disease Education and Referral Center (ADEAR Center). 15 min. (v)

Morgan, Richard L. *From Grim to Green Pastures: Meditations for Sick and Their Caregivers.* Nashville, Tenn.: Upper Room Books, 1994. (b)

My Mother My Father. Chicago, Ill.: Terra Nova Films, 1985. 30 min. (v)

My Mother My Father: Seven Years Later. Chicago, Ill.: Terra Nova Films, 1991. 42 min. (v)

Oliver, David B. And Sally Tureman. *The Human Factor in Nursing Home Care.* Binghamton, N.Y.: The Haworth Press, Inc., 1988. (b)

Padula, Helen. *Developing Adult Day Care.* Washington, D.C.: The National Council on the Aging, Inc., 1983. reprint 1992. (b)

People with Aging Parents. Video #3 of "The Family Matters" series. Nashville, Tenn.: UMCom Productions. 25 min. (v)

Rob, Caroline and Janet Reynolds. *Helping Older Friends and Relatives with Health and Safety Concerns.* Boston, Mass.: Houghton Mifflin Publishers, 1992. (b)

Ross, Steven. *The Caregiver's Mission: A Comprehensive Practical Guide on Caring for Your Elderly Parent, Spouse, or Family Member.* Plantation, Fla.: Distinctive Publishing, 1993. (b)

Sharing the Caring: Adult Day Care. Washington, D.C.: The National Council on the Aging, Inc., 1992. 18 min. (v)

Smick, Timothy S. and James Duncan, et.al. *Eldercare for the Christian Family.* Dallas, Tex.: Word, Inc., 1990. (b)

Sommers, Tish and Laurie Shields. *Women Take Care: The Consequences of Caregiving in Today's Society.* Gainesville, Fla.: Triad Publishing Company, 1987. (b)

Starkman, Elaine Marcus. *Learning to Sit in Silence: A Journal of Caretaking.* Watsonville, Calif.: Papier-Mache Press, 1993. (b)

Struyk, Raymond, J. And Harold M. Katsura. *Aging at Home: How Elderly Adjust Their Housing without Moving.* Binghamton, N.Y.: The Haworth Press, Inc., 1988. (b)

Yale, Robyn. *Developing Support Groups for Individuals with Early Stage Alzheimer's Disease.* Baltimore, Md.: Health Professions Press, 1995. (b)

You and Your Aging Parents. EcuFilm: Liquori Productions. 30 min. (v)

Zweck, Brad. *Parenting Our Parents.* Minneapolis, Minn.: Community Intervention, Inc., 1988. (b)

FAITH DEVELOPMENT AND INSPIRATIONAL

A Good Old Age. Nashville, Tenn.: UMCom Productions, 1989. 23 min. (v)

All Your Parts Don't Wear Out at the Same Time. Baltimore, Md.: Mass Media Ministries. 28 min. (v)

Bianchi, Eugene C. *Aging as a Spiritual Journey.* New York: Crossroad Publishing Co., 1985. (b)

Face of Wisdom, The: Stories of Elder Women. Series of 8 videos. Franciscan Communications, 1993. 27 min. each video. (v)

Fischer, Kathleen. *Winter Grace: Spirituality for the Later Years.* Mahwah, N.J.: Paulist Press, 1985. (b)

Fowler, James W. *Becoming Adult, Becoming Christian: Adult Development and Christian Faith.* San Francisco, Calif.: Harper & Row, 1984. (b)

Gaining A Heart of Wisdom: Finding Meaning in the Autumn of Your Life. Fort Wayne, Ind.: Willowgreen Productions. 36 min. (v)

Hickman, Martha Whitmore. *Fullness of Time: Short Stories of Women and Aging.* Nashville, Tenn.: Upper Room Books, 1991. (b)

Hutchison, Frank. *Aging Comes of Age.* Louisville, Ky.: Westminster/John Knox Press, 1991. (b)

Live Long and Love It! Arcadia, Calif.: Win Arn Video Production. (v)

McCall, Edith. *Sometimes We Dance Alone: Your Next Years Can Be Your Best Years!* Brooklyn, N.Y.: Brett Books, Inc., 1994. (b)

McKee, Patrick and Heta Kauppinen. *The Art of Aging: A Celebration of Old Age in Western Art.* New York: Human Sciences Press, Inc., 1987. (b)

Minnie Remembers. Adapted from the Donna Swanson poem of the same name. Baltimore, Md.: Mass Media Ministries. 5 min.(v)

Morgan, Richard L. *I Never Found That Rocking Chair: God's Call to Retirement.* Nashville, Tenn.: Upper Room Books, 1992 (b)

_____. *No Wrinkles on the Soul: A Book of Readings for Older Adults.* Nashville, Tenn.: Upper Room Books, 1990 (b)

Thibault, Jane Marie. *A Deepening Love Affair: The Gift of God in Later Life.* Nashville, Tenn.: Upper Room Books, 1993. (b)

Thone, Ruth Raymond. *Women and Aging: Celebrating Ourselves.* Binghamton, N.Y.: Harrington Park Press, 1992. (b)

Valentine, Mary Hester. *Aging in the Lord.* Mahwah, N.J.: Paulist Press, 1994. (b)

Welch, Elizabeth. *Learning To Be 85.* Nashville, Tenn.: Upper Room Books, 1991. (b)

MINISTRY, THEOLOGY, AND ETHICS

Aging Me ... Aging You: The Journey of a Lifetime. Louisville, Ky.: Presbyterian Church (USA), 1994. 32 min. (v)

Age Wave ... Wake Up Call. Arcadia, Calif.: The Institute for American Church Growth. 13 min. (v)

Arn, Win and Charles Arn. *Catch the Age Wave.* Grand Rapids, Mich.: Baker Book House, 1993. (b)

Campbell, James A. *What Do You Say?* Nashville, Tenn.: Discipleship Resources, 1991. (b)

Clements, William M., ed. *Ministry with the Aging: Designs, Challenges, Foundations.* San Francisco, Calif.: Harper and Row, 1989. (b)

Clergy: The Gatekeepers for the Future. Washington, D.C.: American Association of Retired Persons. (b)

Even These May Forget (Alzheimer's Disease: A Pastoral Care Challenge). Pittsburgh, Pa.: University of Pittsburgh, Alzheimer's Disease Center, 1991. 18 min. (v)

Even to Your Old Age. Washington, D.C.: The National Council on the Aging, Inc., 1993. 13 min. (v)

Gentzler, Richard H., Jr. *Designing a Ministry By, With, and For Older Adults.* Nashville, Tenn.: Discipleship Resources, 1993. (b)

Good Place to Grow Old, A. San Francisco, Calif.: American Society on Aging, 1991. 32 min. (v)

Hendrickson, Michael C., ed. *Role of the Church in Aging. Volume One: The Implications for Policy and Action.* New York: The Haworth Press, 1986. (b)

_____. *Role of the Church in Aging. Volume Two: The Implications for Practice and Service.* New York: The Haworth Press, 1986. (b)

_____. *Role of the Church in Aging. Volume Three: The Programs and Services for Seniors.* New York: The Haworth Press, 1987. (b)

Hilton, Bruce. *First, Do No Harm.* Nashville, Tenn.: Abingdon Press, 1991. (b)

How to Have an Effective Senior Adult Ministry. Arcadia, Calif.: The Institute for American Church Growth. 30 min. (v)

Hynes, Millie R. *Ministry to the Aging*. Collegeville, Minn.: The Liturgical Press, 1989. (b)

Kemper, Kristen, ed. *Golden Opportunities: Older Adults and the Church*. Brea, Calif.: Educational Ministries, Inc., 1992. (b)

Koenig, Harold G. *Aging and God: Spiritual Pathways to Mental Health in Midlife and Later Years*. Binghamton, N.Y.: The Haworth Press, Inc., 1994. (b)

Koenig, Harold G. and Mona Smiley, et al. *Religion, Health, and Aging*. New York: The Haworth Press, 1988. (b)

Kerr, Horace L. *How to Minister to Senior Adults in Your Church*. Nashville, Tenn.: Broadman Press, 1980. (b)

Linking Your Congregation with Services for Older Adults. Alexandra, Va.: Catholic Charities USA. 17 min. (v)

Maitland, David, J. *Aging as Counterculture*. New York: The Pilgrim Press, 1991. (b)

Moody, Harry. *Ethics in an Aging Society*. Baltimore, Md.: The Johns Hopkins University Press, 1992. (b)

Paul, Susanne S., ed. *A Ministry to Match the Age*. New York: General Board of Global Ministries, 1991. (b)

Paul, Susanne S. And James A. Paul. *Humanity Comes of Age: The New Context for Ministry with the Elderly*. Geneva, Switzerland: WCC Publications, 1994. (b)

Payne, Barbara and Earl D. Brewer, eds. *Gerontology in Theological Education: Local Program Development*. New York: The Haworth Press, 1989. (b)

Preparing for an Aging Society: Changes and Challenges. Washington, D.C.: The National Council on the Aging, Inc., 1994. (b)

Preparing for the Graying of a Congregation. Philadelphia, Pa.: Committee on Older Adults, Union of American Hebrew Congregations, 1995. (b)

Robb, Thomas B. *Growing Up: Pastoral Nurture for the Later Years*. Binghamton, N.Y.: The Haworth Press, Inc., 1991. (b)

Sapp, Stephen. *Light on a Gray Area: American Public Policy on Aging*. Nashville, Tenn.: Abingdon Press, 1992. (b)

Seeber, James J., ed. *Spiritual Maturity in Later Years*. Binghamton, N.Y.: The Haworth Press, Inc., 1990. (b)

Swenson, Harriet Kerr. *Visible and Vital: A Handbook for the Aging Congregation*. Mahwah, N.J.: Paulist Press, 1994. (b)

Vogel, Linda J. *The Religious Education of Older Adults*. Birmingham, Ala.: Religious Education Press, 1984. (b)

SOCIAL SCIENCES, HUMANITIES, AND RESEARCH

Aging America. Washington, D.C.: U.S. Department of Health and Human Services, 1991. (b)

Aiken, Lewis A. *Aging: An Introduction to Gerontology*. Thousand Oaks, Calif.: Sage Publications, Inc. 1994. (b)

Barrow, Georgia. *Aging, the Individual, and Society* (5th edition). St. Paul, Minn.: West Publishing Co., 1993. (b)

Bond, John and Peter Coleman, eds. *Aging in Society: An Introduction to Social Gerontology*. Newbury Park, Calif.: Sage Publications, Inc., 1990. (b)

Bronte, Lydia. *The Longevity Factor*. San Francisco, Calif.: Harper and Collins, 1993. (b)

Brubaker, Timothy H. *Later Life Families*. Newbury Park, Calif.: Sage Publications, Inc., 1985. (b)

Bull, C. Neil, ed. *Aging in Rural America*. Newbury Park, Calif.: Sage Publications, Inc., 1993. (b)

Coming of Age in America, The. Washington, D.C.: The National Council on the Aging, Inc. 30 min. (v)

Dychtwald, Ken and Joe Flower. *Age Wave: The Challenges and Opportunities of an Aging America*. New York: Bantam Books, 1990. (b)

Fried, Stephen, Dorothy Van Booven and Cindy MacQuarrie. *Older Adulthood: Learning Activities for Understanding Aging*. Baltimore, Md.: Health Professions Press, Inc., 1993. (b)

Gerber, Jerry and Janet Wolff, et. al. *Lifetrends: The Future of Baby Boomers and Other Aging Americans*. New York: The Stonesong Press, Inc., 1989. (b)

Growing Old in a New Age. 13 videos in a series on aging. The University of Hawaii, Center on Aging. 1993. 60 min. each video. (v)

Jackson, James S., Linda M. Chatters and Robert Joseph Taylor, eds. *Aging in Black America*. Newbury Park, Calif.: Sage Publications, Inc., 1993. (b)

Jernigan, Homer and Margaret Jernigan. *Aging in Chinese Society: A Holistic Approach to the Experience of Aging in Taiwan and Singapore*. Binghampton, N.Y.: The Haworth Press, Inc., 1992. (b)

Newman, Sally and Steven W. Brummel. *Intergenerational Programs: Imperatives, Strategies, Impacts, Trends*. Binghamton, N.Y.: The Haworth Press, Inc., 1989. (b)

Peterson, David A. *Facilitating Education for Older Adults*. San Francisco, Calif.: Jossey-Bass Inc., Publishers, 1983. (b)

Pifer, Alan and Lydia Bronte, eds. *Our Aging Society*. New York: W. W. Norton and Co., 1986. (b)

Spacapan, Shirlynn and Stuart Oskamp, eds. *The Social Psychology of Aging*. Newbury Park, Calif.: Sage Publications, Inc., 1989. (b)

Thompson, Jr., Edward H., ed. *Older Men's Lives*. Thousand Oaks, Calif.: Sage Publications, Inc., 1993. (b)

Turner, Barbara F., ed. *Women Growing Older*. Thousand Oaks, Calif.: Sage Publications, Inc., 1994. (b)

Vierck, Elizabeth. *Fact Book on Aging*. Santa Barbara, Calif.: ABC-CLIO, Inc., 1990. (b)

Williams, Janice Lake and Janet Downs. *Educational Activity Programs for Older Adults*. New York: The Haworth Press, 1984. (b)

ENDNOTES

CHAPTER ONE

1 Eugene C. Roehlkepartian, *Exploring Effective Christian Education:An Inventory for Congregational Leaders* (Minneapolis, Minn.: Search Institute, 1990), p. 21.
2 *A Profile of Older Americans: 1995* (Washington, D.C.:American Association of Retired Persons, 1995), p. 1 (information based on data from U. S. Bureau of the Census).
3 Elizabeth Vierck, *Fact Book on Aging* (Santa Barbara, Calif.:ABC-CLIO, Inc., 1990), p. 5.
4 *A Profile of Older Americans: 1995,* p. 2.
5 Elizabeth Vierck, *Fact Book on Aging,* p. 8.
6 *A Profile of Older Americans: 1995,* p. 3.
7 Ibid., p. 4.
8 Ibid., p. 8.
9 *Aging America:Trends and Projections,* p. 108.
10 Vierck, p. 96.
11 *A Profile of Older Americans: 1991,* p. 4.
12 Ibid.
13 Ibid., p. 10.
14 Ibid.
15 Georgia Barrow, *Aging, the Individual, and Society* (4th ed.; St. Paul, Minn.:West Publishing Co., 1989), p. 25.
16 Ageism relates to the negative attitudes and practices that lead to discrimination against people simply on the basis of their age.
17 Sara Arber and Jay Ginn, *Gender and Later Life* (Newbury Park, Calif.: SAGE Publications, Inc., 1991), p. 35.
18 Paul B. Maves, *Faith for the Older Years* (Minneapolis, Minn.:Augsburg Publishing House, 1986), p. 19.

CHAPTER TWO

1 Wayne Teasdale, "The Mystical Dimension of Aging," *Aging: Spiritual Perspectives,* ed. by Francis V.Tiso (Lake Worth, Fla.: Opera Pia International, Sunday Publications, 1984), pp. 224–225.
2 Albert Camus, *The Myth of Sisyphus* (New York:Vintage Books, 1995), p. 3.
3 Erik H. Erickson, *Childhood and Society* (New York:W.W. Norton & Co., Inc., 1963).
4 Leo Missinne, "Christian Perspectives on Spiritual Needs of a Human Being," *Spiritual Maturity in the Later Years,* ed. by James J. Seeber (Binghamton, N.Y.: The Haworth Press, Inc., 1990), p. 151.
5 Simone de Beauvoir, *The Coming of Age,* trans. by Patrick O'Brian (New York: Warner Books, Inc., 1973), p. 116.
6 Loren B. Mead, *Transforming Congregations for the Future* (Bethesda, Md.:The Alban Institute, Inc., 1994), p. 90.

CHAPTER THREE

1 The "first age" being childhood and youth and the "second age" being the work productive years.
2 Robert L. Katz, "Jewish Values and Sociopsychological Perspectives on Aging," *Toward a Theology of Aging*, ed. Seward Hiltner (New York: Human Sciences Press, 1975), pp. 135–150.
3 Union of American Hebrew Congregations, Committee on Older Adults, compiler, *Preparing for the Graying of a Congregation* (Philadelphia, Pa.: Union of American Hebrew Congregations Committee on Older Adults, 1995), pp. 3–5.
4 The bold print is by the authors of this book.
5 Union of American Hebrew Congregations Committee on Older Adults, *Preparing for the Graying of a Congregation*, pp. 4–5.
6 Ibid., p. 5.
7 This material is quoted from the National Clergy Leadership Project to Prepare for an Aging Society, a project of The National Interfaith Coalition on Aging, and is copyrighted and reproduced with the permission of The National Council on the Aging, Inc., 409 Third Street S.W., Washington, DC 20024.
8 Ibid.
9 Henri Nouwen and Walter Gaffney, *Aging, The Fulfillment of Life* (Garden City, New York: Doubleday and Company, Inc., 1974), p. 4.
10 Ibid., p. 10.
11 Reuel L. Howe, *Live All Your Life!* (Waco, Tex.: Word Books, 1974), pp. 23–40.
12 Van Tatenhove is the Frank Bateman Stanger professor of pastoral counseling and chair of the Department of Pastoral Ministry at Asbury Theological Seminary, Wilmore, Kentucky.
13 Melvin A. Kimble, Susan H. McFadden, James W. Ellor, James J. Seeber, editors, *Aging, Spirituality, and Religion: A Handbook* (Minneapolis, Minn.: Augsburg Fortress, 1995), pp. 417–428.
14 Ibid., p. 417.
15 Ibid.
16 Ibid.
17 Ibid., p. 418.
18 Ibid., p. 419.
19 Ibid., p. 420.
20 Ibid.
21 Ibid., p. 422.

CHAPTER FOUR

1 Loren B. Mead, *Transforming Congregations for the Future* (Bethesda, Md: The Alban Institute, Inc., 1994), p. 41.
2 Peter M. Senge, *The Fifth Discipline: The Art & Practice of the Learning Organization* (New York: Doubleday, 1990), p. 206.

CHAPTER FIVE

1 Walter H. Moeller, *The Older Person, the Church, and the Community* (Indianapolis, Ind.: Indiana Commission on the Aging and Aged), pp. 10–11.

CHAPTER SEVEN
1   *Model Statement on Caregiving* (Washington, D.C.: National Interfaith Coalition on Aging, 1988), p. 2.
2   Nancy R. Hooyman and Wendy Lustbader, *Taking Care of Your Aging Family Members* (New York: The Free Press, 1988), p. 3.
3   Ibid., p. 4.
4   Ibid.
5   Elaine M. Brody, "Women in the Middle and Family Help to Older People," *The Gerontologist* 21, 5 (1981): 471–480.
6   *Adult Children and Aging Parents* (Atlanta, Ga.: Presbyterian Office on Aging), p. 1.
7   Ibid.
8   *Model Statement on Caregiving*, pp. 3–4.
9   Nancy R. Hooyman and Wendy Lustbader, *Taking Care of Your Aging Family Members*, p. 5.

CHAPTER EIGHT
1   *Intergenerational Projects: Idea Book* (Washington, D.C.: American Association of Retired Persons, 1993), p. 7.
2   Edward A. Powers, "Diversity Enriches Us All: Programming for All Ages," *Can We Uplift the Spirit as the Body Slows Down?* (Washington, D.C.: National Interfaith Coalition on Aging, 1993), p. 3.

CHAPTER TEN
1   Ken Dychtwald and Joe Flower, *Age Wave: The Challenges and Opportunities of an Aging America* (New York: Bantam Books, 1990), p. 11.
2   Elizabeth Vierck, *Fact Book on Aging* (Santa Barbara, Calif.: ABC-CLIO, Inc., 1990), p. 5.
3   Jerry Gerber and Janet Wolff, et. al., *Lifetrends: The Future of Baby Boomers and Other Aging Americans* (New York: The Stonesong Press, Inc., 1989), p. 17.
4   Ken Dychtwald and Joe Flower, *Age Wave: The Challenges and Opportunities of an Aging America*, p. 20.
5   Ibid., p. 10.
6   Vierck, *Fact Book on Aging*, p. 5.
7   Loren B. Mead, *Transforming Congregations for the Future* (Bethesda, Md.: The Alban Institute, Inc., 1994), p. 17.
8   Ibid.
9   Peter M. Senge, *The Fifth Discipline: The Art & Practice of the Learning Organization* (New York: Doubleday, 1990), p. 4.
10   Loren B. Mead, *Transforming Congregations for the Future*, p. 103.
11   Jerry Gerber and Janet Wolff, et. al., *Lifetrends: The Future of Baby Boomers and Other Aging Americans*, p. 245.
12   Ezra Earl Jones, *Quest for Quality in the Church: A New Paradigm* (Nashville, Tenn.: Discipleship Resources, 1993), p. 47.